A Year Outside of Time

Titus Naso

Tomis Press

A Year Outside of Time
Titus Naso

Copyright ©2023 by Titus Naso

All rights reserved. No part of this publication may be reproduced, performed, or stored in a retrieval system, or transmitted in any form or by any means, without the written permission of the publisher.

This book is a derivative work based on a larger work previously copyrighted under the title, "Annum Poetica," Copyright ©2021 by Titus Naso.

Published by Tomis Press
Silverton, Oregon

Hardcover ISBN: 978-1-958337-00-4
Paperback ISBN: 978-1-958337-14-1
E-book ISBN: 978-1-958337-15-8

Titus Naso is a pen name of Jesse S. Smith.

titusnaso.com • tomispress.com • jessesmithbooks.com

Poetry / Current events / Personal Growth

Introduction

At the height of the pandemic lockdowns, I was reading *Fasti*, a collection of poems about the Roman calendar and holidays written by the poet Ovid, who was exiled to Tomis on the Black Sea by the Emperor Augustus Caesar in the early years of the Common Era, two millennia ago. Inspired by Ovid's work, I challenged myself to write a poem a day for the next year. As my project progressed, Ovid became my mentor, and my poem-a-day project helped me through a historic year of turmoil and change on many levels.

This selection of personal and political poems tells the story of one rural parent's life during an unforgettable, historic, momentous year. It's a story of social isolation, personal transformation, distance learning, racial awareness, civil unrest, political turmoil, and natural disasters, all while the Covid-19 pandemic ravaged the whole world. Throughout the year, Ovid and other literary figures from the past are seen as mentors and guides.

We begin in April of the year 2020.

~Titus Naso
March 31, 2022

April, 2020

An Inauspicious Beginning
4-21-20

Grey are the clouds in the dreary Spring sky
though the leaves ev'rywhere are brilliant green
and I do not think we can expect rain.
I have been reading Ovid's *Fasti* poems,
and I wish I had read them earlier,
for they suit my int'rest in calendars.
Ovid speaks of soaring themes in his work:
gods and heroes, rulers and warriors,
historical events of great moment.
Always my concerns are more personal:
I hope you will find me "relatable" –
my concerns, I believe, are typical.
I find myself educating children
and ill-suited to the occupation
in this era of Corona Virus
when the schools are all closed for quarantine
and all the country is closed for business.

Resolving on the spur of the moment
to begin yet another new project,
most impulsively I have decided
to write each day a poem, for the next year;
and have perhaps rashly repurposed this,
my artsy notebook I had been saving,
intended for the rough draft of a book
of historical fiction I shall write
someday, starring great Hannibal Barca.
But alas, no great general am I.

Never shall I lead elephants across
high mountain passes, besiege enemies,
or destroy their armies of trained soldiers
with double-enveloping maneuvers.
Instead, the thrust of my day is concerned
with trying to get two kids to focus;
an impossible task, like Sisyphus:
as soon as it's done, it begins anew.

Today is not auspicious to begin
this new project of mine; but should I wait
and attempt to start it next New Year's Day,
I would inevitably botch it all,
forget to start it, or overthink it.
'Tis better to begin than plan too long.

So join with me, dear reader, and journey
on this adventure 'round the Sun once more.
It will be int'resting to discover
how long I can sustain daily entries,
and how much life will have changed by the end.

Turning Thoughts
4-22-20

Just as when a man a new lover finds
he can't keep the thought of her from his mind
but upon her image his mind returns
as for her company his spirit burns
and he imagines the things they will do
to fill one another with pleasure true –
almost as eagerly my thoughts have turned
to this new project; well, perhaps not "yearned" –
with eagerness considered this new task
I've set for myself (no one else would ask),
and imagined what I might choose to say
in a year of writing a poem a day!

A Day in the Life
4-22-20.ii

It rained this morning, and my run was slow.
I only got about four hours' sleep.
The dog is acting up, the sky drizzles,
and the children are procrastinating:
a bad habit they learned from me, I'm sure.
But Younger showed initiative today
when he completed a phonics worksheet
without being prompted; and for his part,
Older has a video conference
scheduled with his History class, to present
his project on castles, still incomplete;
I need to interrupt his Lego play.

Project complete, his meeting has adjourned;
the day's school work done, the kids watch TV.

The Grocery Run
4-22-20.iv

I made an afternoon grocery store run.
Always an important part of my week,
it has taken on new significance
in the era of Corona Virus
with such shortages of essential goods
as my generation has never seen.
We try to limit our trips in to town
and maintain proper social distancing
to avoid spreading the deadly virus.
I wore a face mask; such is my future:
but the store had flour, the first time in weeks.

Disaster Life
4-27-20

Both of my children have ADHD
and I struggle with issues of my own.
This weekend, both their prescriptions ran out.
Without medication, today was hard.
My six-year-old screamed and hit his brother,
menaced him with a gardening shovel,
threw toys down the hallway, coins 'cross the room;
promised he would stop, then did it again.
I do not feel like much of a hero.
I barely endure, and struggle with tasks,
overwhelmed, messy house, disaster life.
I'm lucky my wife tolerates me.

The Creek Walk
4-29-20

We walked down to the creek this eve,
enjoyed a pleasant moment there.
The birds were singing in the trees
and fragrant scents perfumed the air.
The grass was wet from earlier rain,
the evening warm as day more fair.

From mess and fuss we need a break,
a quiet moment's peace to take.
We should go down there every day,
it really is not far away
and only takes a little time
and always brings such peace of mind;
though clouds of grey mimicked my cares,
which chase me 'bout like Furies fierce
whose whips and torches give no rest,
and calm times with their shrieks do pierce!
Sadly, that's what my mind does best.
And truth to tell, it is a fact
that oftentimes I do distract
myself with books or Internet;
they don't always help me forget
the ancient and most haunting pain
that's seared its pathways 'cross my brain
just like an ancient mariner's map,
'X marks the spot, here is the crap!'
Left to myself, always the same,
my thoughts go right back there again...
But Nature brings perspective back,
fills up with beauty what I lack.
So blessings on the trees and stream,
this life, better than any dream;
and fittingly for my dark brain,
the ev'ning now has turned to rain.

Walpurgisnacht
4-30-20

A new beginning April's last day is,
it opens up a doorway to next month.
Rather than close a door upon the last,
this day invites us to enjoy the next,
like Christmas Eve when children lie awake,
but set in Springtime. This is Beltane Eve,
Eastern European Walpurgisnacht.
The merry month of May will meet the morn,
the joyful verdant month of high repute,
much mentioned in the madrigals of old,
the month associated with heroes
like Robin Hood, who Sherwood Forest strolled,
and good King Arthur who with knights so bold
held feasts and jousting for the Whitsunday:
now Pentecost it's called, this year it falls
upon the last day of the month of May.
So greetings, merry May, we welcome you;
with open arms and joyful gaze we smile.
Great thanks we give to April as it ends
and brings us into May, like a good friend
who drives us to another friend's party;
a friend who, though most welcome, cannot stay.

May, 2020

My May Queen
5-1-20.iv

My May Queen
my sweet love
wide eyes
dark hair
luscious curves.
My May Queen
my sweet love
my wife.

My May Queen
my sweet love
gentle
caring
warrior woman.
My May Queen
my sweet love
my wife.

The Fool
5-5-20

Today we were blessed by the sun,
the grass it was wet on my run.
My children, prone to distraction,
and I, the responsible one,
barely got through our assigned tasks
although very little was asked.
They worked on their projects for school,
while I wrote that I am a fool
as poems and lyrics I compiled.
Collected, these reveal my style:
developed by journal writing,
it's confessional and biting,
a little too open and raw:
I fear readers will drop their jaw
not awestruck by beauty, but shock,
when I bluntly say the word "cock,"
or when I true stories do tell
that some say condemn me to hell.
With good fortune I have been blessed
and nobody will be impressed
by all the mistakes I have made
as my life goals became waylaid
and forgotten over the years;
hence all of my poems about tears.
It traces back to a dark time
when I was young, only 'bout nine;
but my failure to overcome
is all that's important to some.
They say, "Many endured abuse
  much worse, so you have no excuse!"

That's fine, I don't want to compete,
but without it, my tale's incomplete:
I was broken by that dark past
long before Twitter mobs harassed.
But now I've decisions to make:
do I still discuss my mistakes?
I have an instinct to explain;
it gets me in trouble again.
It's better to focus on themes
of high adventure, and of dreams,
of great leadership, and ideals,
not just losers spinning their wheels,
'though all my tales of my mad youth
are just rehearsals of the truth.
It's now time to set my sights high,
achieve something before I die.
I tell myself that I will try
as grey storm clouds menace the sky.

A Sunny Day
5-8-20.ii

Not merely sunny is today
so send children outside to play.
The weather's nice, nothing to fear,
it's the warmest day so far this year!

The Murmurs of the Mob
5-12-20

An excerpt from Chaucer's *Clerk's Tale*,
my own translation, may justice prevail.

O rav'ning mob, unstable, full of lies!
Turbulent, changing like a weather-vane!
Delighting to spread rumors new and sly,
but like the moon, ever you wax and wane.
Always you're full of shit-talking, inane,
false judgment and hypocrisy pursue.
Only a total fool listens to you!
It's now the worst it's been in all our age,
their murmurs slay my heart and my courage.
For to my ear come hurtful words: a voice
so cruel that it my aching heart destroys.

Rhododendron Flowers
5-17-20

A-buzzing are the bees that fly about
the blossoms of the rhododendron bush,
the flowers fully opened now, fancy,
a brilliant bright color cacophony:
riotous radiant red, pretty pink,
luscious lavender, wholesome white, glowing
illuminated by bright beams of sun
to them giving a glow of godlike grace,
the huge heads of these fresh flowers us uplift.

Math Homeschooling
5-19-20.ii

Helping my six-year-old with his math homework
the thought occurs, the column structure shows
arithmetic's Arabic origins:
for the ones column is there on the right;
we add things or subtract them right to left
just as Semitic language is written,
but kind of backwards for our culture.
If we had derived basic math concepts
the ones place would be over on the left
and we would solve problems from left to right!

A Visit from Family
5-22-20

Family visits! A welcome change today --
O familiar faces, you who traveled
so far to see us were surely welcome.
We're unaccustomed to such long absence,
even though we live at a great distance;
but this Corona Virus quarantine
has isolated us from family,
a separation of many long months.
We gathered not at Easter time this year,
nor did we meet for Grandma's birthday love.
Though distance has been forced between us long,
our hearts always remain close through the years.
Should virus keep us quarantined yet more,
still family we'll be, and thoughts keep us close!

Fortuna
5-25-20

O fickle Fortune of folly and fame,
goddess of luck, and of random chances,
a gambling man may curse or praise your name,
as do lovers pursuing romances.
We see how one newly favored prances;
but when you turn your back, their head hangs down!
When blessed by Fortune, every hour dances;
when Fortune turns away, we wear a frown.
Thou, Fortune, hast the public abandoned to drown.

Intrusive Thoughts
5-26-20.ii

I wonder if the minds of other folks
do not subject them to intrusive thoughts:
the constant barrage of terrible things,
guilt and shame and obsession with failure,
constant reminders of everything wrong;
never a moment's peace, truly not one.
It's always there, always interrupting,
spoiling the enjoyment of happy days,
ruining what should be perfect moments.

"Just don't think about it" is not helpful.
You think I *want* to think about this shit?
You try not thinking about a hammer
that's loudly pounding on a sheet of brass,
insistent, constant, ringing and noisy,
pounding, pounding within your very skull,
defiling all that's beautiful in life.

Birthday Regrets

The big problem with having my birthday:
it's a reminder of my wasted life,
the opportunities I've thrown away,
the failures and squabbles and wretched strife,
the many promising years, now long gone,
and for myself, I have nothing to show.
The subject's not fruitful to dwell upon,
my chances grow slimmer daily, I know.
But on the plus, my family rallies round,
they build me up with their love and support.
My sister wrote a poem that did astound,
made me tall when I had been feeling short.
Although the vultures may be circling up above,
my family shows me the way forward with their love.

Coping
5-29-20

It's time to cope with Adult ADD
and a whopping dose of anxiety.
I seem to suffer social phobia;
occasionally hypomania
throws a switch that turns on my depression;
it is not fixed by learning a lesson.
At the core of it all, PTSD,
self-diagnosed, but very real to me.
If it's possible, with great elation
I'd welcome a fix through meditation.

The Approaching Storm
5-30-20

I heard the storm approach from far away,
it marched from up the valley, ominous,
like legions of invading army troops
the thunder rolled with booming bursts of sound
as cannons and destruction havoc bring;
it shook the house while yet 'twas far distant
and promised fury to unleash as soon
as front arrived, and upon us descend.
Then soon enough it did so, and the rain
beat down upon the house, the trees, and land
while all the birds to fleeting shelter took,
and under covers huddled wife and I.
The windows open we had left all night
for evening's air had been so stifling hot.
The sun has shone upon us this last week
in all its glory as the Solstice nears.
Now all the land's refreshed with breezes cool
and thirsty plants are grateful for the rain.
The storm has passed, although grey clouds remain,
it promises to be a gentle day.

Black Lives Matter
5-30-20.ii

I write about my petty concerns
while in the news headlines, the world burns.
The protests are based on issues of race,
a serious problem in this time and place.
Saying "Black Lives Matter" should not be
a sentiment that arouses controversy.
It seems obvious that they're people, too,
regardless of color, just like me and you.
Change does not come from peace and quiet...
but *here*, it's mostly White folks at the riot.
The closing message for you and me:
let's work to bring about equality.

The George Floyd Protests Continue
5-31-20

'Twould self-indulgent be to write of aught,
when all the land is in such great uproar,
else it were racial discrimination
and brutal police officer actions,
of which the murder of George Floyd unarmed
is just the latest outrage we have seen,
the unjust death of another Black man.
The time is right for late-night mass protests.
We can't deny, some want to see it break.
If this gets worse, things could get out of hand.
I hope our country notice now will take,
and implement reforms throughout the land.

June, 2020

Admiring Nature
6-1-20.iii

I stand here on the banks of flowing creek
admiring flowers, butterflies, and birds
on the first day of June, early summer.
All Nature is bright, and filled with great hope
while my dog looks expectant, and wonders
why I delay when there's so much to see.

This Moment in Living History
6-6-20

There are so many things to write about,
but only one subject is relevant
to this moment in living history:
and that is racial inequality,
the racial injustices in our world,
police brutality and violence.
Too many Black people have been murdered
by police officers for no reason.
Too many white people clearly don't care;
their attitude adds insult to the pain.
Why should it be so difficult to say
that Black Lives Matter? It's self-evident,
but someone always offers quibbling words:
and that in itself should tell us something.
The greatest goals for our society
are tolerance and mutual support,
equality of opportunity,
freedom regardless of sex, race, or creed.

We must resolve to see our own mistakes
to learn from them, and improve every day.
We must admit our country's racist past
and present, and try to change the future.

Mud
6-9-20

"mud slows me down" I wrote
in my smartphone fitness tracker app's hist'ry note
reflecting, I saw, on a deeper level it's true:
for spiritual mud slows me down, too

Make America Great At Last
6-10-20

Amazing that the protests continue,
crowds march against police brutality.
Already, assumptions under review
as we confront racist society.
Power to the people! Land of the free,
together working, change we can create.
Build social welfare, defund the police;
we rise together with love, reject hate:
these protests will make America truly great.

June in Haiku
6-14-20 and 6-15-20

birds sing in the trees
only aware of the now
night's rain storms have passed

sun shines on the grass
the day is cheerful and bright
last night, the storm raged

the sky is cloudy
drought no longer worries us
the grass is happy

A Pleasant Stroll
6-15-20.iii

The evening sun was so pleasant that I
went for a stroll without destination
to feel the sunbeams shine upon my face
and to enjoy the coolness of the air.
Around the corner, to the fence post's end
walked I, while serenaded by the birds.
This truly is a wondrous land of bliss.
Though weeds have grown wild-tall with all this rain,
I love how nature-close our farm life feels.

Filing Taxes During a Pandemic
6-17-20

When he is grown, I want my son to be
a man of whom the whole world will be proud:
responsible, filled with integrity,
with kind and gentle thoughts full well endowed.
These traits then must I demonstrate: behave
to with my good example my son teach
so he won't grow to emulate a knave;
no, I have got to practice what I preach.
Towards this end, my focus for this day
was sitting at my desk, papers to sort,
so that the family taxes I might pay,
and worry not about going to court.
Adventures of this kind no glamour offer us;
living stable life offers future wondrous.

Into Summer
6-21-20

Family my greatest blessing is!
Good fortune truly looks like this.
With wife I'm raising two great kids;
by Universe we have been kissed.

The insects chirp and birds do sing
as into summer from the spring
the seasons turn, and with them we
stay open to the happy things.

On these focus our intellect,
not on shit from the Internet,
or clouds, or stress, or squabbling kids,
just change the focus to forget.

Aesculapius
6-22-20

O Aesculapius, god of medicine
in Corona Virus time we hail thee!
Help us the health of people to promote,
encourage them to begin wearing masks
that help to lessen deadly virus spread,
and let science be depoliticized.

A Curse
6-26-20

The error is in thinking that when you
attack another person, call them names,
you are positioning yourself nicely:
that calling someone else "bad" makes you "good."
But nothing could be farther from the truth!
Descending to the level of insults
places you on a level with the low:
debased, defiled, cruel; a spreader of lies,
smears, slanders, and hate. Popularity
is not worth such dirt on your precious soul.
May all your ugly words fall back on you,
crush you beneath their weight a thousand-fold.

The World's Throne
6-29-20.iii

Looking upwards at the sky of blue
the wind blows through the trees of green
orange flowers bloom for me and you
most beautiful we've ever seen

The rippling current of the stream
that flows between banks over stones
If everything's indeed a dream,
then wherever you sit is the world's throne.

But What Legacy?
6-30-20

Just as Philip of Macedon unto
his son, great Alexander, did impart
the will to conquer, along with a plan,
and most important, a well-trained army;
even so did Hamilcar the Barca
bequeath to Hannibal forces, purpose,
and a plan for the invasion of Rome.
To my sons I leave a lifetime of dreams
with no plan for capture: only the chase.

The Whispering of the Shades

Inspired by Dante's *Purgatorio*, Book I.115-130 and Book V.10-21
6-30-20.iv & .v

My Guide indicated the dewy grass
whereon I stretched myself with grateful tears
as he cleansed me of that all-cov'ring grime
that had clung to me as I traversed Hell.

"Why allow your mind to be fixated
  to the point that you lose momentum?"
my Guide asked me crossly. "Why does it matter
  to you what these Shades whisper here? Come on.
Always, people will talk. You must let them.
A man who becomes mired in his own thoughts
loses sight of goals. Worry blunts purpose.
Stand as tall and sturdy as a mountain,
whose peak sways not in the mightiest wind."

July, 2020

Celebrate our Cherished Ideals
7-2-20

The theme of the month is patriotism
but it's not the theme of the year.
Our "cancel culture" so obsessed with flaws,
no one is supposed to appreciate
incremental progress, cherished ideals,
speeches and banners that founded this land
because our Founding Fathers failed to solve
the problem of slavery, our great shame.

I won't argue. It is a valid point
that American democracy first
excluded more people than it included:
women, the poor, Native peoples, and Blacks.
And slavery, accepted under law,
is a great stain upon our history.
(To make things worse, from today's perspective,
 patriotic fervor and flag-waving
 are well embraced by such modern fascists
 as in ev'ry generation return.)

And that's a shame; because we should always
accept a cause for celebration
when we can find one: make the most of it!
We can celebrate our cherished ideals
even as those have evolved over time.
As flawed as Independence may have been,
it was a step in the right direction
down the long and winding road to Freedom,
Justice, Equality, and Equity.

Incremental change is based on power,
and limited by compromise always.

When the just lack the power to defeat
the wicked full resoundingly, for good,
then we are forced to compromise with them
to achieve anything, and pursue goals.
The alternative is to be ruled by them:
unacceptable, I think you'll agree.

No matter which side of the fence you're on,
many folks are probably wicked, to you.
There may be truth in that, we all have flaws;
but let's not focus on reasons to hate.

Most "bad guys" have redeeming qualities;
all real-life "good guys" have character flaws.
Let us come together and celebrate
our common ideals, if we can find them.

Exiled to Tomis
7-6-20

Sent far away to barbarian lands,
to distant Tomis, shores of the Black Sea
among the Goths, the exiled poet stands,
his heart filled with a yearning to be free,
his mind filled with the injustice of it all.
Sent away from his home into exile,
he does what poets do: begins to write.
Protestations keep him busy the while:
he scribbles elegies into the night.
He got in trouble for something he said:
Augustus was outraged by poems of love!
Perhaps he's fortunate not to be dead
he thinks, looking upon the stars above.
He was accused of something else: we don't know quite
what his sin might have been, whether severe or trite.

Likely a squabble, drama quite petty,
resulted in his becoming outcast.
The "reason" is not the real reason, when he
was made a symbol. He would be the last:
none else would challenge the morals rigid
after Augustus had laid down the law.
The onlookers decided to be frigid
when scapegoated Ovid's fate they all saw.
No one stood up for him, he had no defenders,
and his poems arrived in Rome, *non grata* sender.

Cancel Everyone
7-7-20.ii

I had originally intended
to spend the month of July writing poems
about the founding of America,
our guiding principles and our ideals,
and those historical events which led
at length to independence from Britain.
But every time I check social media
it's filled with endless vicious, righteous hate
portraying historical compromise
as a deep fundamental betrayal
of those very principles we hold dear.
I am tired of the fight, it never ends.
If you "cancel" everyone who ever
made a mistake or disagreed with you,
eventually you'll cancel everyone
without exception: even your own self.

Part of a Team
7-8-20.ii

It's lonely to stand alone 'gainst the world
with every man's hand always against you
      like Ishmael.
It brings hope to hear words of agreement,
support, or even that rarest, friendship:
      part of a team.

The Mouse
7-10-20

I have many ideas
  but I did not sleep well;
my mind is a fog,
  my other project is Hell.
Of it I've now written
  eleven thousand words,
though none will be smitten
  by my awkward verse.
The sun it is bright
  this morning in July,
and my son just discovered
  a mouse who recently died.

One Hundred Thirty-Five Thousand Dead
7-11-20

Apocalypse meanwhile rages all 'round;
the death toll, one hundred thirty-five thousand,
and people pretend it's not happening:
they say Corona Virus is a little thing;
they act like it's an onerous task
just to wear a simple face mask.
And so the virus spreads,
people die in hospital beds:
the old, the young, the middle-aged,
while the squabbling public stays outraged
and nothing gets done
under the July sun.
Situation worse,
I believe we're cursed.

Tax Extension
7-13-20

It's a fucking nightmare to calculate tax!
Oxymoron is "Paperwork Reduction Act."
I've spent days on these calculations.
It's an exercise in frustration.
Too bad this is the best way we've thought of
to fund our great nation.
Normally, would have been due in April
to much sorrow;
due to Corona Virus, we got an extension until
the day after tomorrow.

Broken Heart Syndrome
7-14-20

Being separated from other people
is quite stressful to the body and mind.
Separation and isolation are
effective, even cruel, punishment forms.
Both Ovid, exiled to distant Tomis,
and Sir Thomas Malory, to prison
confined for the rest of his lonely life,
describe suffering from grievous illness.
The body is connected to the mind,
thus stress and loneliness can make one sick.

Confinements during the virus outbreak
have led to a significant increase
in what experts call "Broken Heart Syndrome."
There was an article on CNN:
documented cases of heartbreak death
as separation causes suffering.
It seems sorrow and loneliness can kill.
When Lancelot felt "his heart would to-brast"
there was a real risk it might truly stop!

Thus all the people living
          so far apart
are physically hurting
          in their hearts.
Corona Virus rages
          and meanwhile
we all are trapped and distant
          like exiles.

Sandcastles
7-17-20

Like a child building a wall of wet sand
and hoping to keep out the rising tide,
or trying to hold water in cupped hand
but none of the droplets will stay inside;
just like a man who's trying to find work,
try as he might, there's no work to be found,
everyone he talks to calls him a jerk
and dashes his dreams into the ground:
we struggle and try, and keep pressing on,
tho concept we pursue just isn't right;
we're trying to keep singing the wrong song
after the band has walked off for the night.
It's time for us all to learn to work *together*
and function all the time – not random, like weather.

Happiness from Moment to Moment
7-17-20.ii

Like a child who's playing in the sand,
not caring she a futile task pursues;
or a man with fortune in his hand –
well, at least he enjoys singin' the blues!
True happiness in life is not a goal:
you feel it from moment to moment in your soul.

How to Provoke Even More Civil Unrest
7-19-20

Now the Administration does provoke
civil unrest, near: in Portland, Oregon,
where unidentified officers are
jumping out of unmarked vans and grabbing
people off the streets, and detaining them
with neither due process nor evidence.
These are police state dictator tactics
employed against peaceful demonstrators –
it's the opposite of democracy.
It's as though this is a dress rehearsal,
next step: authoritarianism.

Cut Off
7-19-20.ii

Shunning has been a religious practice
as long as religious law's been set down:
book of Genesis, Seventeen : Fourteen
says that if any man's uncircumcised,
"that soul shall be cut off from his people" –
he shall be cast out for personal choice,
the group's arbitrary will enforced
by constant threats, and the fear of shunning.

The Creek in July
7-20-20

And now the summer sun is high
above us in the clear blue sky
     the air is warm
     the bugs do swarm
this is the essence of July.

While Seven throws rocks in the water
on shore I sit, wond'ring if it will get hotter.
Two months ago, the spot where I now park my butt
was underneath the springtime's raging flood.

The rocks forming the banks of this our stream
are tumbled willy-nilly, quite obscene;
they know firsthand just what erosion means
and ask us if life really is a dream.

Now Seven, hopeful, has expressed a wish
to catch for himself one of the small fish.
He stands so still, then splash! a rock he throws.
Alas, he has yet to catch the minnows.

Then picks up the blessed breeze
rustling through the restful trees
which languidly drop a few green leaves
into the creek, to float out to the seas.

The breeze is past, the air is still,
envy the fishes with their gills
who swim beneath the waters clear
while my skin burns in the sun up here.

On the surface I skip a rock,
but Seven asks for me to stop.
He bravely has courage to say,
"Dad, don't scare the fish away!"

Dragonflies and yellow jackets,
edit notes in their square brackets,
call to me across the years
as my notebook's wet ink smears.

The Land of Hypocrisy
7-24-20.ii

I'm watching an Egyptian sitcom now,
streaming on Netflix. It is quite funny.
It's called, *The Land of Hypocrisy*.
The scenery reminds me of the year
when I lived there, it all still looks the same!
Tall concrete apartment buildings with shops
at street level; same cars, same clothes, same signs.
Characters eat *koshary* as take-out;
that was always one of my favorite parts.
The show itself at first seemed to pose questions
about morality and social life,
but has degenerated (well, for now)
into a transgressive heist scenario.

The Yellow Jacket Nest
7-26-20

It's hard to focus my mind
   on the thoughts that are best.
Today, I exterminated
   a yellow jacket nest.

Biblical Heroes
7-27-20

When I read the Bible
  the heroes I see
are the ones who weren't treated
  kindly by history:
Like Esau, the better brother,
  by his own family undermined;
or Shechem, foully murdered
  then slandered for all time;
or Eve, whose painful punishment
  surely did not suit her crime.

The Coyote
7-29-20

This morning on my run,
      a coyote crossed my path.
The special sight was fun.
      The thing that made me laugh,
the beautiful animal
      crossed so close in front of me
I had time to say, "Hello,"
      but my dog, he did not see.

He looked up and around
when he heard my voice sound.
A greeting to the coyote I did say,
but my dog turned to look the wrong way!

As the coyote ran off to my right,
      my dog, next to me, looked left.
The coyote escaped quite:
      he'd have got away with theft!

My dog realized too late
      and followed to the fence;
but the coyote, like a wraith,
      had vanished: he knew not whence.

So he ran back o'er to me
      and we proceeded on our jog;
running, like the coyote, to be free,
      just me and my dog.

The Rabbit
7-29-20.ii

I will tell you a little of myself.
I live so far out in the countryside
that my driveway is surprisingly long.
This evening, while dragging out to the street
my trash and recycling carts down the drive,
they made so much noise, I could not listen
to my podcast; and my aching right toe
with the broken toenail was pushing up
against the edge of my boot as I walked
hauling these trash cans out to the roadside
and thinking to myself, "This life is it.
  This is the best life I could ask for.
  This is the life I have chosen to live.
  This is the best life I could ever have.
  The rest of the details are up to me.
  Whatever has not worked yet: up to me.
  Mistakes I'd rather forget: up to me.
  The sunset is coming this way; up to me
  to bring color to this day, and live free.
  Whatever details are left are my own,
  details I still have to deal with someday;
  but I am a man full-grown;
  I'll figure it all out in my way.
  There always seems to be one detail
      out of grasp –
it's not the first time, and you've already failed
      at this task.
But the motivational speakers
     still want you to believe
everything you dream of
     you can still achieve

       if you just ask:
  let success shine down from above
  and in the glow of universal love
      you will bask."

I left the cans out by the road,
and began to walk home, quiet without my load.
While walking, I was thinking all these thoughts
about this strange path through life that's my lot,
when I was quite surprised to see
a rabbit in my path – coney!
A skinny one at that, scrawny,
and brown, with fluffy tail shown me.
But that was later – first, it hopped up near
to investigate me, showing no fear,
as close to me as I am now to you,
an experience of what in life is really true:
a moment, when all the Universe is born anew,
      and another
      and another
      and another
in an infinite cascade,
reflected and mirroring beyond
our comprehension, into the realm
of pure abstract imagination:
formless
nameless
timeless
bodyless
beingness.

August, 2020

Lunasa (Lammas)
8-1-20

...
The ancients made sacrifice a symbol
of what we would call "abundance mindset" –
the faith, belief, and certain knowledge
that the harvests to come through this season
will be abundant harvests bringing joy;
preparing the mind for awesomeness,
preparing gardens, weeding to work well,
and filling the spirit with gratitude
that brings life joy, and makes one pleasant company.
On solar Wheel of the Year calendars,
Lammas is the Summer Cross-Quarter Day
in between the Summer Solstice, Litha,
and the Autumnal Equinox, Mabon.

Lammas blessings upon you, dear reader;
may you enjoy the bounteous gifts of Lugh.
May your sacrifice and your gifts come back
in blessings a thousand-fold upon you!

The Height of Summertime
8-2-20

The month of August: named for Augustus,
the Emperor who thought he was a god,
this is the very height of summertime,
when cloudless is the sky of blue above.
The days are so hot we hide in the shade;
the sunshine is bright, winter worlds away.
The heat is so intense, some leaves get parched and brown;
yet joy is so immense, this month wears the year's crown.

Yesterday's Rain
8-7-20

The rippling water sound in the stream bed
and cheerful birds in branches overhead
the warm summer sun and the clear blue skies
yesterday's rain showers and chill breeze belies.

Vibrations
8-8-20

We know not how others our words affect
as each of us is struggling through our days
obsessing over what's true and correct.
Vibrations ripple out in many ways
from each and every message that we send
as we with others do communicate;
what they hear's not always what we intend,
so patience and love we must demonstrate.
I was inspired, and perhaps I was scared,
by a story a friend recently confessed
about how the mind really will "go there"
when a person is sufficiently distressed.
But a simple word of encouragement well-timed
can be enough to change another's frame of mind.

Though calling out public bad behavior
was not in fact my initial intent
when I sat down to write, on this day here:
still, down the rabbit hole my dark thoughts went.
I soon began of bad habits to speak
whereby we people spread feelings of hate
by calling others "narcissist" or "freak" –
putting others down makes nobody great.

With words of condemnation and judgment,
some find that hurting others is their power.
We must ask ourselves, "Is that what I meant?
And is it worth dwelling on these thoughts sour?"
Even my poem from its intended topic strayed:
through habit and complacency, mistakes are made.

A Shooting Star
8-9-20.iii

I saw a shooting star tonight
maybe everything will be all right.

Take a Moment
8-10-20

'Tis the season to live in the moment:
let go of the past, and future worries;
release anger and resentment and pain.
Allow all negativity to float
away into the clear blue summer sky,
and listen to the breeze blow through the leaves.
Feel the warmth of the sunshine on your face.
Enjoy each breath. Take a moment to be.

Just Be
8-14-20

I've heard a lot of advice,
a little of it from people wise;
but focusing on my breath has never worked for me,
so this morning I tried the mantra, "Just be."
When I focus too much on my breath,
it gets all wonky and feels like death.
This has forced me to face the facts:
thoughts of breathing don't help me relax.
But inner peace is important to find;
I need a way to clear my mind.
By concentrating on my "Just be" mantra words,
I may be able to eliminate mental turds.

Tampering with the Mail
8-16-20

It's not often that we have a chance to watch
the government intentionally botch
the upcoming election important;
not such a surprise, there have been portents
such as its viral pandemic response,
logical people met with threats and taunts.
Someday historians will tell the tale
of Presidential assault on the mail,
'cause Trump is so afraid that he will lose
if people are allowed to vote and choose.
I have been alive for forty-five years
and never experienced such great fears
of imminent civilization collapse:
aye, my faith in humanity doth lapse.

A Worthwhile Effort
8-18-20

It makes me feel like a terrible Dad
to force the kids out of the house – so bad!
But soon as at the creekside we arrived,
Seven saw a beautiful butterfly.
It makes the effort seem worthwhile
if the memories will raise a smile.
Now Seven's reading a Garfield book
while Fourteen throws stones in the brook,
something for the dog to chase
here and there, from place to place.

The Rabbit's Demise
8-20-20

I met the friendly rabbit
   on the very same day
when the quiet brown coyote
   silently crossed my way.

The rabbit hid in the brambles,
   the coyote ran under the fence,
and I have not seen
   either one of them since.

But the coyote has been around,
   I can tell, I've seen its "sign,"
whereas the rabbit, I fear,
   has moved on to realms divine.

For it was just a week later,
   I spotted along the drive
an indication that the rabbit
   might no longer be alive.

'Twas in the selfsame spot I'd met the rabbit
   in the driveway: I noticed there,
a copious pile of coyote shit
   containing another animal's hair.

And I've seen more coyote scat since then,
   it's looking after its own needs:
but now, the turds it leaves in my jogging path
   are filled with naught but blackberry seeds.

The Nutria
8-29-20

The nutria looks like a small beaver,
but it has a long thin tail like a rat,
         as though some sick mad scientist
         exploring his brain's mental twist
chopped two animals with a cleaver
and sewed them back together like that.

Sometimes, Forgiveness is Hard
8-30-20.ii

I forgive you
I forgive you
I forgive you
It's hard
It's hard
It's hard
I forgive you
I forgive you
I forgive you

September, 2020

Focusing My Mind
9-1-20

It's sunny on this, September's first day.
My child and I explore the stream bed
and I try to focus my mind on months,
displace social media hate narratives.

Hooting Back and Forth

I am the owl hooting in the tree,
and you, the other owl, call back to me.
We call to one another near and far,
of one another think where'er we are.
We hoot to one another, back and forth.
Our chicks squawk to us, attention demand.
Our love gives direction, pointing true North,
for one another, our family, the land.
My daily focus is here, the nest,
while you go hunting, searching for your prey –
and there the metaphor breaks: you're the best
at helping others all day every day.
If birthdays are celebrated by birds,
I hope yours is beautiful beyond words!

The Baby Eaters
9-3-20

Rather than by their values positive,
far too many online communities
are brought together by their narrative
about some scary perceived enemies.
People are brought together by villains
at whom they sling their shameless blatant lies.
"The facts no longer matter," say your friends,
"the out group is so bad, we must be right!"
Their enemies are easily accused
of eating babies, or of crimes much worse.
Their *own* behavior, they claim, is excused:
"Drive out the evil *other*, so accursed!"
To heal our world and make it truly great,
we must define ourselves by love: not hate.

"Observe!"
9-4-20

There once was a man named Lucretius
who was not being facetious
            when he said, "I shall show
            all we think that we know:
observe what Mother Nature can teach us!"

A Breathing Meditation
9-5-20.ii

breathing in
  I feel the warm sunshine on my face
breathing out
  the breeze blowing down the beach cools my skin

Mandatory Evacuation Orders
9-8-20

The area where we live is under
mandatory evacuation orders
due to the proximity of a fire
that's burning down the forest and, wind-blown,
rampaging across the dry countryside.
The summer is always dry, but these days
thanks to the scourge of global climate change
the land is parched and dry and super hot;
and all the frantic bracken which grew up
so quickly with the ample rains last spring
has now become brittle tinder, kindling
to feed the fire and amplify its heat.
We're hoping, hoping, hoping that this is
an excess of caution: all will be fine,
the fire will take a different direction
and we'll be able to return home soon.
My heart goes out to those who have lost all,
even as I hope we will not join them.

Passing the Time
9-12-20

I helped my brother-in-law paint his house
to pass the time while I'm a refugee.
There's hope the fire will come under control
and we'll be able to return home soon.
This evening, we watched the movie "Mulan,"
a great tale of female empowerment.
...

Returning Home After the Danger Has Passed
9-16-20.ii

We've returned to the house
  though the air is still bad.
This is one of the strangest
  experiences I've had.

The house is still a mess
  but I feel pretty wiped.
I sure would just like
  to call it a night.

Easy to Say, But...
9-19-20.ii

"Renew aspirations? Be your best self?"
Easy to say, but my house is a mess
and my children are disobedient;
I have no career; I piss people off
whenever I open my mouth to speak;
and I take offense, rather than ignore
the constant insults, slights, and snide remarks
which other folks feel entitled to make
more or less constantly, but won't accept
in return, when it's directed at them.
Gods, people piss me off, they really do.

Catullus
9-20-20

"*Odi et amo*," Catullus once wrote,
"I hate and I love," and the hate comes first,
making Poem 85 relatable.
Catullus is at his most human here,
passionate, tormented, voicing his pain,
speaking for me through his ancient verses.
"I love and I hurt," I also once wrote
an otherwise unremarkable poem
decades before I heard of Catullus,
"and it fills me up inside," it went on,
"I love and I hurt and it tears me apart,"
echoing Catullus, though I knew not.
"*Fieri sentio et excrucior*,"
Catullus concluded in his own work:
"I feel its onset, and it torments me."
These feelings may not be universal,
but I know I share them with a poet
who died more than two thousand years ago,
and somehow feel a little less alone.

Two Hundred Thousand Dead
9-21-20

Two hundred thousand Americans have
died as a result of Covid-19.
The deadly Corona Virus rages,
and millions believe it is just a hoax –
"It's not so bad, it's not worse than the flu,"
they say, "we should not have to wear a mask
  or stand distanced from other people
  or avoid crowded events and places
  or any of these other things we're told."
And resulting from willful ignorance
perpetuated by the government
(to cover the Trump administration's
 tepid and inept response to the threat)
and by conservative media, too,
(deny reality, prove loyalty)
this attitude kills thousands every day;
the numbers grow worse as schools re-open,
yet people still remain in denial.

Mabon
9-22-20

Mabon, the son who was stolen away
from Modron the Mother in years long past
has lent his name to this Equinox day
reminding us he was rescued at last
by Arthur the King and his knights so bold
acting upon ogre's evil behest.
They sought near and far, in those days of old,
to fulfill magical mystical quest.
Recorded in Mabinogion, the tale
inspired writer Aidan Kelly to choose
lost, found Mabon's name, and it has prevailed
as the name most modern Pagans now use
when we call forth our Equinox blessings
and unto the Goddess our voices sing.

Recent News Items
9-25-20

Just a few recent items from the news:
a White Supremacist shot at police
today, and died when they shot back at him.
They were just trying to write a ticket,
because that's how police get their money:
though "wanted," they were not looking for him.

Instead, police try to shut down protests,
declaring them unlawful assemblies
despite that most pesky First Amendment.
Invoking early city-wide curfews
provides them an excuse to make arrests
before protesters even misbehave.

It's just the sort of abuse of power
the protesters are in the streets about:
the dictatorial police squadrons
operating with no accountability.
They broke down the door of a woman's house
while she was trying to get a night's sleep,
and murdered her, although she was unarmed.
Breonna Taylor, essential worker,
nurse and decent person with a future,
was killed by police for no good reason,
and they face no consequences at all.

This week the President has grabbed headlines
for vowing to hold onto the office
even if his opponent wins the vote;
because Trump and the party that backs him
just do not believe in democracy.

All this distracts from Corona Virus,
which has killed more than two hundred thousand
in the United States alone so far,
and still it shows no sign of slowing down,
response from leadership: ineffective.

The wildfires, worsened by global warming,
are only partially contained so far,
and only thanks to recent days of rain
are we able to go outside unmasked.

To top it off, the Supreme Court justice
Ruth Bader Ginsburg has died of cancer.
Casual hypocrisy on display:
opportunist Republican Party
pretended to care about principles
when they blocked President Obama's judge;
but now that they are the ones in power,

they have no principles, just naked greed,
and fully intend to ram their own through.

All this is just the news from the past week.
That's why I'd rather write about Ovid.

Change
9-26-20

It does not occur at a constant pace:
sometimes too slow, sometimes a frantic race,
sometimes too much, more often not enough.
Although the very thought fills some with fear
there's been an awful lot of it this year
and more is coming! and it may be rough.
The world around us often seems quite strange:
rather than fear it, let us welcome change.

Online School
9-27-20

The school year begins almost a month late
this year, due to pandemic and wildfire.
I'm certain that my kids will both do great
if I can motivate learning desire.
About the format I'm still hesitant:
thanks to the virus, school is all online.
Left to themselves, my kids are indolent;
when I try to motivate them, they whine.
I don't know if I will get much support
from distant online teachers of their class.
I fear that in time tempers will run short,
and online school be a pain in the ass.
I'm experiencing trepidation
about my children's education.

"Stand Back and Stand By"
9-30-20

In last night's presidential debate,
Trump winked at a group that's based on hate.
    He told the Proud Boys to "stand by"
    and surely it is quite clear why:
he thinks White Supremacy makes America "great."

October, 2020

A Celestial Conjunction
10-2-20.ii

The Moon and Mars are in conjunction tonight
careless in the night sky, shining bright.

October in Haiku
10-3-20

small rips in blue jeans
red scratches on arms and legs
we trimmed bramble vines

ii.

green leaves fade to brown
red and gold drop from the trees
fall is upon us

iii.

Scrabble and stories
guacamole for dinner
a family evening

iv.

Halloween costumes
knitting creativity
my wife is brilliant

v.

such ironic news
denial helps spread the disease
Trump has caught Covid

A Society of Trolls
10-6-20

We're entering a social era new
thanks to advances in technology.
Our heads are full of bullshit the trolls spew:
to hurt enemies, they lie cheerfully.
They'll say anything to cause painful harm,
they want to ill the world with rot and stink:
from basement-dwellers to Russian troll farms,
their purpose is to poison how we think.
Yet still, most people think "It's just a joke,"
and join in laughing at today's target
as all around the world goes up in smoke:
brotherly love we are told to forget.
Troll hatred seeps into everyone's minds
and gets worse, the more time we spend online.

Ovid in Exile at Tomis
10-7-20

I'd love to write a script for a movie
about Ovid at Tomis in exile.
Although the *Tristia* poems name no locals,
they tell a distinct story of despair:
the poet, sick and gaunt, depressed, crazy,
complains about his life, pisses folks off –
they do not like to hear their town slandered!
But near the end he must stand in defense,
joining the lines to repel barbarians;
and at the last, he is joined by his wife,
long-suffering and loyal to her man,
she joins him in his exile, far from Rome,
and only then does he feel he is home.

Celebrate the Dark
10-8-20

It is no myst'ry why this time of year
has long been associated with fear,
for all around the plants wither in death
and in the Northern climes you see your breath.
All 'round the land is rotting in decay,
the dampness, rain, and mold fill each wet day.
The spiders build their webs across the path,
then end up in our face, we scream with wrath.
Our houses invaded by mice and rats,
in evening we are dive-bombed by the bats.
So nat'rally our thoughts turn to the grave,
its terrors from which none are truly saved.
Instead we learn to celebrate the dark:
dress up, get festive, and give life some spark!

Always to Seek
10-9-20.ii

I would not have for inner peace to quest
if it was something I at first possessed.
I would not need for balance still to strive
if it was simply part of being alive.
But it is my nature always to seek –
that's who I am, it's not just some mystique!

Never Cease
10-10-20

"No one believes in me, 'cause I have failed!"
the old man moaned, he sniffled, and he wailed.
"No matter if I in myself believe,
  the world shall ne'er offer me a reprieve:
  for people love to judge and to condemn;
  and once they start, there's no escaping them.
  If I should someday meet with some success,
  they'd chase me down to tell me I'm a mess!
  It's too late now, I cannot over start,
  so I must find acceptance in my heart."
Then started he again, heaving a sigh.
Despite it all, he'd never cease to try.

Book the Second
10-11-20

Welcome, dear reader, welcome back!
     The poems continue on:
I am the book they're written in,
     I sing to you this song.

Perhaps you're reading a compilation:
     'twas no gap, not a page
'tween the end of that last poem there
     and this – but it's a new age!

For as the author writes in me
     and fills me up with verse
'tis I who shapes the words he writes
     and the stories he'll rehearse.

My pages provide form and size,
     their texture to the hand
imparts a certain reality
     to thoughts both vague and grand.

Yes, on this day the writer has
     begun a new notebook;
yet otherwise, nothing has changed,
     the world is left un-shook.

The one thing I can offer you
     dear reader, (don't be distraught)
is assurance that the author will
     make the best of what he's got!

Hello, It's Me Again
10-12-20

Now writing as myself again,
      I have dropped the pretense
of writing in my notebook's voice,
      I hope that made some sense.

A Fine Fall Day
10-12-20.ii

With my young son I have walked down
      to the creek – and it roars!
All the recent autumnal rains
      have filled it deeper than before;
and now through brush and undergrowth
      he asks me to explore.

The rain has stopped for a little while
      and it's a fine Fall day
for looking at mushrooms and ferns
      that grow along the way.

The Leaders in the Government
10-13-20

Of Corona Virus we live in fear
it has dominated our lives this year –
along with increased racial awareness
with people calling for basic fairness.
Meanwhile, the leaders in the government
care only for power and establishment
as the Senate tries to push a Justice through
who will take away health care from me and you;
meanwhile, Mitch McConnell just laughs and laughs
about the virus relief bill he threw in the trash.
Trump talks endless shit, and no one cares he lied;
meanwhile, hundreds of thousands of people have died.
I know nobody wants to hear what I wrote,
but I hope they will all go out and vote!

Changing the Subject
10-16-20

There really is no way to turn it off.
Perhaps I am not trying hard enough?
The chatter is incessant, and the threads
of arguments go on and on and on
within my mind, no matter what I do.

I focused on my own mantra, "Just Be."
Briefly, my mind almost did clear...
but all too soon distraction came my way;
a symptom of my ADD, I guess.
When I looked up, I was on a tangent,
my meditation I had forgotten!
I prob'ly need to practice a lot more.

A change of subject is my only hope.
I'm better off thinking of others' lives,
of Ovid, Milton, Frost, and Dickinson,
so from my own concerns my thoughts will go
forgetful of the drama for a while.

A Bonfire of Memories
10-17-20

I made a pile of memories
    I wanted to forget,
of stress and shame and ancient pain
    and dreams not come true yet.

I piled them in a jumble,
    I piled them up quite high.
They looked a mess, I do confess,
    but still I had to try.

I set those memories on fire
    and watched them burn away.
Though my brain contains their ashen remains
    I'm free to live a new day.

The Fungi of Fall
10-18-20

The tree could take it no more
and tumbled to the ground
where it was overtaken by spores
which soon sprouted all around.
In time the vibrant mushrooms grew
all o'er the rotting log,
providing us with a grand view
of Nature's catalog.

Fall Deepens
10-23-20

This morning there is frost upon the rails,
for as the Fall deepens, the nights grow cold.
The days grow shorter and the sunlight fails:
summer is gone, the year is growing old.
Some raging storms we have already had,
but this morning it's bright and mostly clear.
Most agree, 2020 has been bad
and nobody is going to miss this year.
Less than two weeks until election day,
the day on which the future we'll decide.
People I know speak of moving away
if fails the vote on which all our hopes ride.
For on that one day so much still depends:
a lot could change before this strange year ends!

Leveraging Hate
10-23-20.ii

Between love and hate, love gets all the praise;
but read the news or scroll the feed these days,
it's soon apparent people won't hesitate
to unify allies by leveraging hate.
Anger and disgust inflame passions strong:
when rage is power, folks will hold it long.
They'll fan the flames with lies, put on a show
to plant the seeds of hate in folks they know,
to ensure that no one will let it go.
It's harder to sustain movements with love,
but try we must, if we're to rise above.

Sad Insights
10-24-20

I looked at old notes from my shelf
and there within I found a wealth
of sad insights about myself,
of inner demons and mental health.

My early poèms tell the tale
of inner screaming, as I wailed –
and just as I had caught my breath
came suddenly face to face with death.

The Goal Achieved
10-25-20

I achieved a major goal today,
and yet that goal's not gone away –
although I've checked it off my list,
I haven't seen the last of it!
Although this battle has been won
(and sometimes it was kind of fun)
completing it was just step one,
I'm never really truly done.
I guess that's why they call it work,
and I don't want to be a jerk
so I have to accept the fact
my goal achieved is just the first act.

It's Time!
10-29-20

The month of October has sure gone fast
       although we know time does not last
On all my work I have fallen behind
       and shadows fall upon my mind
But rather than just sit here and complain
       it's time to go jogging again.

Halloween Eve
10-30-20

Today we're getting in the car
we're going to travel very far
to see my distant family
who are so near and dear to me.
In costume to see and to be seen
for lovely Samhain Halloween
but not to walk up and down the street,
'tis not the year to Trick or Treat –
from Corona Virus we must hide;
we'll probably just stay inside.
I'm sure it will be a lot of fun
but now I've surely got to run!

Halloween
10-31-20

I'm glad we have Halloween
       so close to Election Day.
It helps to distract us
       from the worry and the stress this way.
From my usual social media
       I have my phone logged out.
There are so many much better
       things to think about!

November, 2020

Election Eve
11-2-20

Tomorrow's vote engenders so much angst
it's hard to think about the month of Thanks.
There is a chance on which we've placed our hope –
and there are many people yelling, "Nope!"
Most of us worry more than we confess –
th' election's outcome causes us much stress!

Election Day
11-3-20

We've waited for this day for four long years.
Our daily lives have been so full of fears;
a nation'l mood such as words cannot express:
the Trump years have been such a fucking mess!
We hope things will begin to go our way:
we hope to see a landslide win today!

Being Better
11-5-20

My child screamed, "I hate you!"
"I love you," I replied.
My child screamed, "You're a jerk!"
"I love you," I replied.
For we must be better than them,
tho theirs words wound us inside.

Guy Fawkes Day
11-5-20.iii

Guy Fawkes Day already has its own poem;
thanks to "V for Vendetta," its words are well-known.
Despite the gunpowder treason and plot,
the 5th of November I have forgot!

It seems an odd thing, folks would celebrate
the near-death of all those who legislate –
bespeaks uneasy truce with what we list.
Guy Fawkes was totally a terrorist
who placed gunpowder beneath Parliament
so those leaders would all to Hell be sent.
I hope we can agree, ladies and gents,
that *killing* should not decide the government.

The Long Vote Count
11-6-20

This year's election still has not been called
while in swing states continues the vote count.
How close it has been, we are all appalled:
support for evil in such high amounts!
For "evil" is the best way to describe
the effects which Trump administration
has had, with gross incompetence and lies,
upon the people of this great nation.
But tho the vote was close, we have great hope
the final count at last will go our way.
To reelecting Trump, we have said "Nope!"
America will start a brand-new day.
Four long years, from our fears we've been hidin' –
place we our hopes in President Biden!

Victory!
11-7-20

The happiness is genuine
      as people celebrate.
It has not changed my narrative
      'bout what doth motivate
the people – for a lot of folks
      voted based on their hate.

And hating Trump is reasonable,
      he'd gladly kill us all!
Pursuing his self-serving lies
      he'll tell his tales so tall,
calling Corona Virus "cured"
      while thousands more dead fall.

But hating and governing
      are so far from the same,
and the popular voices on Twitter
      can't move past calling names.
I surely hope my people will
      learn to play a new game!

But Biden and Harris already both
      have risen to this moment in time,
showing a willingness to rise above:
      and frankly, that's a good sign.
Their interest is in getting something done,
      also a priority of mine!

Sore Winners
11-8-20

Today the anger in my feed
is speaking of the people's need
to deal with all the nation's pain –
and things will never be the same!
Yet we must try to understand:
we *have* to unify the land.
For if we look about and see
ev'ryone as an "enemy"
but find no place for "trust" or "friend,"
our opportunity will surely end.

The Same
11-9-20

All humans are just people
      no matter what folks claim.
We talk about "good" and "evil"
      but we're really all the same.

Another Task
11-10-20

I gave myself another task,
I thought it not too much to ask;
for it'd take but a little while...
And so I put it on the pile
of all my tasks not done before,
and tossed them all into a drawer.

Rain and Hail
11-13-20

And now down pours the rain
upon our heads again
and everything is wet
so we shall ne'er forget
that we are fortunate
to live in a green state.

Now fall the hail stones,
the tree trunks sway and groan
and the creek waters rise
like the love that's in your eyes.

The Spectators
11-14-20

I chose a goal quite far away
  and t'wards that goal I ran.
I got lost and I went astray –
  now farther than when I began!

The spectators along the side
  of the course that I took
were gleeful, as they watched me fail,
  and laughed 'til their sides shook.

"You'll never reach that goal, you fool!"
  they jeered with mockery.
"You should not aspire to lofty heights!"
  is the advice they gave to me.

"Just be resigned to your lot in life,"
  said one who *thought* he meant well.
"Improvement is a path to strife,
  you'll find yourself in Hell!"

I glared at him for this advice,
  tho I'd not succeeded yet.
The way he'd phrased those kindly words
  sure sounded like a threat!

A threat indeed – for others heard
  and tried to make it true:
"So, you think you can improve your lot
  in life, asshole? Fuck you!"

They gathered, as I tried to pass,
      for my "friend" had more attention to me drawn.
These others stood there, blocking my path
      to prevent me from moving on!

Now in addition to distance
      and steepness of my trail,
the opposition of my peers
      added to my travail!

Yet still I fought, and still I cursed,
      and gave them an elbow.
"Someday I will better myself,"
      I said, "and you I'll show!"

Then pushing past them through the crowd,
      I continued on my way.
I knew that I could reach my goal
      despite them all, someday.

And though the path was winding, long;
      despite naysaying "friends,"
with steely determination and grit
      I got there in the end!

A Sore Loser
11-15-20.ii

These poems are not intended
        to recite the daily news
else this book would grow distended
        and my mind would blow a fuse.

But it's a point of interest
        and a strange thing to say
that Trump will not concede his loss –
        still calling it "rigged" today.

Staying Out of It
11-16-20

Too civil for the "far Left,"
too egalitarian for the Right;
I am a man without a side
trying to avoid a fight.

A Rainstorm
11-17-20

Today the rain came pouring down
on our house, here outside of town.
It rained hard enough to soak my clothes,
and the Covid mask over my nose.

The storm had many fronts, it seemed
        leading my Seven year old to ask
if it would grow still more intense
        or if the center point had passed.

This evening it has passed indeed:
  the storm cloud, aye, it parts;
and through it, I can see the stars:
  those lights that warm my heart.

Two Hundred Fifty Thousand Dead
11-18-20

Today my lovely wife is sick
  I report with some alarm –
she's spending the day home in bed
  here on our little farm.

And though there are many things that can cause
  all sorts of stomach upset,
the deadly pandemic raging outside
  is something I cannot forget.

For although the alternate reality liars
  try to fuck with everyone's head,
the truth is that Covid-19 has left
  a quarter of a million people dead!

I'm hoping that it's just a cold,
  for hope is what I must –
until we have information,
  hope's where we place our trust!

Luckier Than Most
11-19-20

Even when things go wrong, I'm fortunate;
even in bad times, luckier than most.
I must focus my mind on gratitude
to reflect on blessings, but not to boast.

A Negative Covid Test
11-20-20

Her Covid test was negative
       we learned with great relief.
America's poor attitude
       simply defies belief.
People refuse to wear a mask,
       causing others much grief.

A Growing To-Do List
11-21-20.ii

I push myself too hard
I call myself a bard
I write a daily poem
and try to keep a home:
watch kids, and clean, and cook,
meanwhile writing a book.
By hand I weed the trees
and no one else is pleased –
four hundred plus in ground,
fucking field mice have found
their bark a tasty snack;
so I'll be going back
to the tree sapling store
and plant some hundreds more.
Old titles I re-released
this week, no wealth increased
because I make no sales:
at business I have failed!
Meanwhile my main website
has suffered quite a plight:
I take feature requests,
but don't sign up new guests.
It would be really great
complexities to automate,
but there's just too much to do;
I work alone – too few!
Since help I'll never get
new expectations must I set.

A Network Outage
11-24-20

When I was born, there was no Internet.
When I was in college, e-mail was new.
Interactive websites did not appear
until I was in my mid-late twenties.
My first social media was on MySpace,
sev'ral years before Facebook's ascendance.
But now, in the age of Corona Virus,
we are all distant from one another
and our whole society is online:
our interactions, our entertainment,
our work, our education, even sex
(well, that is, within certain limits, ha!).
I buy holiday gifts, plan vacation,
and pursue my shambles of a career
all on this modern computer network.
My children are learning math and science,
language arts and history, all online.
But today, the Internet did not work.
It took me nearly six hours to upload
a ten-minute video to YouTube,
and Seven lost the connection to his
video conference with his teacher and class.
We live in a beautiful paradise
with trees, and a creek, and an open field;
but the technology infrastructure
is more than twenty years old, and it sucks!
Without broadband, we're cut off from the world.

The Parting of the Clouds
11-25-20.ii

It rained so hard today,
it washed sadness away.
The storm clouds parted, and I'm
ready for a new day.

Thanksgiving Day
11-26-20

Let's fill our minds with gratitude
    and on this day give thanks!
We'll have a joyful attitude
    and stroll the river banks.

We'll feast and join in gratitude,
    bake pie, and roast turkey –
we'll focus mental attitude
    on life, love, and liberty.

It is a season of gratitude
    and thoughts of charity,
as we adjust our attitude,
    think as community.

A Bevy of Quail
11-27-20

I looked! And there, in my back yard
      saw a bevy of quail.
I thought, "Their life is not so hard,
      they know nothing of travail.

"They do not work to meet their needs
      or debate choices with words
They just find the seeds on which they feed
      and mate to make more birds."

But then I had a second thought:
      "Think of the quail's life yet again,
with danger fraught of being caught
      by coyotes, and eaten!"

Blame Comet Neowise
11-27-20.ii

It's sometimes hard to express
and the reader might not really guess:
the pandemic which about us doth rage
is the defining characteristic of our age.
While millions live in silent fear
we stay inside, want out of here,
cast high our eyes, up to the skies,
blame 2020 on Comet Neowise.

December, 2020

Distant Suns
12-2-20

O stars, O stars, bright shining in the sky,
the lights of distant suns so far away
at distances incomprehensible,
a distant blazing mass seen as faint light
a-twinkling through our atmosphere at night.

Welcome, Tree!
12-5-20

A tree we have welcomed into our home,
so bright and fresh with needles of green;
almost as though we were living outside –
but outside it is cold; in here, it's warm!
The tree would have preferred, no doubt, to stay
outside in the cold, in the rain and sun
instead of getting chopped down, a slow death:
we fill its stand with water for freshness.
It is traditional, and so festive;
the tree brightens our hearts in wintertime.

The Mark of Cain
12-12-20

Something physical in the brain
in fact is the true mark of Cain –
        on old ideas of guilt
        our whole system is built,
but that system's unjust, it is plain.

Trump's Election Lies
12-12-20.ii

The daily "current events" overwhelm –
recording them all here is not my job.
It's been so terrible, Trump at the helm
is still trying the election to rob.
He's just making things up, screaming 'bout fraud
and telling lie after lie after lie.
Those MAGA hypocrites with righteous God
would hap'ly do anything for that guy.
It's unreal we find ourselves in this state
with thousands from Covid daily struck dead.
It's what we get for allowing so much hate –
could have had Hillary '16 instead!
Folks think it's funny to be cynical,
but this shit's real, we must be clinical.

Strands of Christmas Lights
12-13-20

The strands of colored lights we love to string
around the house to make the season bright
with all the joy and gladness that they bring
as cheerfully they shine into the night.
On our front porch, around the posts we've wrapped
these strings of Christmas lights, and at the top
more lights we've hung, with staple gun in fact,
'til we ran out, and then we had to stop.
The lights frame our entrance like a bright arch,
the glowing mouth of magic tunnel cave.
I wonder if we'll leave them up 'til March?
I wonder if they'll help Seven be brave?
Red, green, purple, orange, drive away fear
shining through the night, the rest of the year.

The Exception
12-14-20

There's an exception to that rule!
Sometimes we make ourselves a fool
and tell ourselves more lies
when we tend to generalize:
"It's never good, it's always bad,
  this meal is just the worst I've had!"
If we don't want our life to stink
perhaps we must change how we think.

Yule Eve
12-20-20

Now, as the Earth moves closer to the Sun
begins the coldest time of the whole year
for us, up in the Northern Hemisphere –
seasonal paradox of atmosphere,
and of the planet's tilt on its axis
(more powerful than orbital variance).
Although the tilt is greatest Solstice day,
the atmosphere retains autumnal warmth...
but wintertime grows colder: watch for snow!
The very shortest day of the whole year
is the day on which we say winter starts –
the Winter Solstice, coming tomorrow!

Tragic News
12-20-20.ii

My poèm's message is one of good cheer:
dark nights will soon begin to grow shorter!
But there's another thought here in my mind;
within my social circle, tragedy:
my cousin's best friend's wife just killed herself.
I don't know the details; they don't matter.
It's the dark winter of a long dark year.
My heart goes out to everyone who knew her.
So hold your loved ones tight, and keep them close,
and offer your support as best you can.
We often don't know another's struggles.

Winter's Chill
12-22-20

Though winter's chill's arriving late this year,
a shiver tells me that at last it's here.
  Tonight may freeze
  my old man knees
and just in time: Christmas is now quite near!

Head On Spike
12-23-20

Am I the source of my own stress?
Sometimes my life is such a mess.
I say things that piss people off –
a pattern, when repeated oft.

In sooth, I wish to be well-liked;
yet here I am, with head on spike.
To have opinions contrary
is a recurring trait for me:
which, when you know, it's plain to see
this common trait of ADD.
In person I am often meek,
I don't intend to conflict seek;
and yet, if I were quite all right
I'd never get into a fight
with strangers on the Internet
who hold a grudge they'll ne'er forget
and yet accuse me of the same.
Although they barely know my name,
they relish some strange rumor heard
and point a finger at the turd
who tweeted as a parody
after he was parodied on TV.

Christmas Day
12-25-20

You don't have to believe in Virgin Birth
or magic star that guided Three Wise Men,
to offer up a prayer for Peace on Earth
and love to fam'ly'n friends from way back when!
The caroling, the feasting, and the gifts,
the tree, the decorations, and the lights
bring us good cheer and our spirit uplifts,
making this day beloved from morn 'til night.
So strike the chord, and come on, sing along
with one of those old tunes that we all know.
I'm sure you have a fav'rite Chistmas song
about chestnuts, and loved ones, and the snow!
I'm not a member of the faith, it's true,
but I'll wish a Merry Christmas to you!

The End of a Terrible Year
12-28-20

The year draws to a close,
      our thoughts turn to the next;
our feelings at this time,
      hard to set down in text.

Due to Corona Virus
      we all have lived in fear,
and with Trump in the White House
      fascism seemed too near.

Now hope is drawing closer
      than for years it has been
with Joe Biden's ascendance
      and first doses of vaccine.

For such a long time, the world has been
      falling apart at the seams –
we've all gotten out of the habit
      of focusing on our dreams!

Draws 2020 to an end
      and none will shed a tear
Look we now forward to
      an excellent New Year!

Frost
12-29-20

There's so much frost upon the ground
feet walking make a crunching sound.
It grows up from the grass like hair
and the back porch is slick, beware!
At first glance, if you did not know
you might mistake it for light snow
(but then no matter how you felt
 by midday all the frost will melt).

Moonlight Through Clouds
12-30-20

So thick and grey they obscure the sky
       and yet there's light to see.
'Tho stars be hid by the clouds up high
       the moonlight's enough for me.

January, 2021

New Year's Day
1-1-21

Today at last a New Year has begun,
it is a time for symbolic fresh start.
We shall go forth in search of joy and fun
and try to put some gladness in our hearts.
With each New Year our lives begin again
symbolically, marked with resolutions.
We tell ourselves that we'll improve by then,
inner lives undergo revolutions.
A time of change is a time to improve,
it's such a time when calendar renews.
We can decide to fill the world with love,
we can decide to be the selves we choose.
We stride t'wards hope ahead, leave fears behind,
and hope to control destiny with our minds.

A Power Outage
1-2-21.ii

A storm came by, with random fury bent
upon destruction, and a tree branch sent
      into our local power line –
      you know, we had been doing fine
'til of a sudden, out our power went!

An Invocation
1-3-21

They have returned at length, auspicious days
described by Ovid in his *Fasti* poems.

O! Great Ovid, guide my pen and my thoughts
as I contemplate Roman calendars,
and help me to make clear to modern folks
how much we have in common with folks of old:
reveal continuity of culture.

Uprooting Blackberry Vines
1-3-21.iii

A sunny day after a heavy rain
is good for uprooting blackberry vines,
the best way to ensure they won't come back.
When soil is damp, the grasping tangled roots
can be dislodged, with effort and a will.
Be sure to wear long sleeves and burly boots,
and heavy gloves to grip the thorny vines!

The Capitol Insurrection
1-6-21.ii

And now, an insurrection has begun!
We should not be surprised by these events.
The MAGAs have been working t'wards it now
throughout the long years since twenty-sixteen.
They do not believe in democracy;
that's why for Trump they voted, after all.

They told us all along they'd not accept
election results, unless their guy won –
we cannot be surprised they won't accept
election results, now that their guy lost.
Today they stormed the Capitol Building
in Washington, D.C. – no mere protest,
an act of insurrection violent!
The Joint Chambers were into hiding forced,
prevented from confirming vote tally:
doing the bidding of the "President"
who holds himself above the law, always.

Another "first" occurred, after all that:
Facebook and Twitter accounts suspended!
We long have wondered if they ever would
take such a step. It's a relief to know,
disturbing 'tis that it has gone this far.

Assassinated Caesar was the first
of a long line of Emperors of Rome;
his death did not restore democracy.
It's not something we wish to emulate.
Our peaceful transfer is what makes us great –
we still can save it; it is not too late.

The Turmoil of Our Times
1-7-21

The turmoil of our times, rising ascent
perhaps has peaked with yesterday's events
but if it's over, only time will tell –
I'll let you know if we descend to Hell.
Truth, justice, and the American way?
Democracy is still alive today!

They Pretend They're Shocked
1-8-21

Perhaps, if my country is fortunate,
there will be little in the news of note
for the three months remaining of my "year"
and all my future poems in this volume
will be focused upon petty concerns,
those trivial details of my daily life
such as consume most people's attention:
business, relationships, my goals and plans,
workout routines and homeschool trivia,
and retellings of Ovid's *Fasti* poems,
mixed in with modern holidays of note,
the distant movements of the stars and Moon,
such random observations as arise.
I dearly would prefer that future course
to insurrection and new Civil War
such as Trump and his supporters would like.
No peace or freedom would satisfy them –
they want democracy quite overthrown!
They have always preferred dictatorship,
they made that clear almost six years ago
when to the "Trump Train" they leant their support:
racist, misogynist, illiberal,
elitist, anti-health-care Donald Trump.

Inciting rioters to storm Congress
in hopes of preventing election loss
was quite in keeping with his character.
It is exactly who he's always been:
a wannabe Augustus Emperor,
enabled by those sycophantic fucks
whose goals mostly aligned with all of his
but now pretend that they're shocked! Oh, so shocked!

"How could he do what he has always done?"
This was a low point for America:
may we all learn from our mistakes henceforth,
resolving to do better evermore.

Debating Articles of Impeachment
1-13-21

'Twas on this day the Roman Senators
bestowed the title of Augustus to
their Emperor, at the Republic's end,
and with great celebrations they all cheered
the man whose army ended Civil War
(tho he himself was sickly and fought not).

'Tis on this day in our Republic now
the *second* time Congress has brought debate
upon the Articles of Impeachment
our wannabe emperor to remove
from the office of the Presidency:
for trying to incite a Civil War.
That asshole Donald Trump has never had
good reason to be in that office grand:
democracy he does not comprehend,
aggrandizement is all he cares about.

Across the Pass
1-14-21

Where we live, the weather's mild
a perfect place to raise a child.
Across the pass, the winter's cold,
a perfect place for growing old.

Remembering Dr. King
1-17-21

This year it must mean more
after all that's gone before
as we remember Dr. King
from shore to shining shore.

It's a day of great import
and let us not sell it short
as we remember leader great
it's okay to cavort

His ideals we celebrate
yet we still hesitate
policies to implement
that would make our country great

We must work t'wards equality
it's no accident, you see:
it will take work from you and me
in the land of the free.

Four Hundred Thousand Dead
1-19-21.ii

'Tis Trump's final day in office at last;
a grim milestone our sad country has passed.
It's largely because Donald Trump has lied
that four hundred thousand people have died.
It is the saddest way to be ahead:
no other country has so many dead.

Inauguration Day
1-20-21

Hooray! Inauguration Day – rejoice!
To era new on this day we embark.
In joyous song people lift up one voice.
The contrast could not be any more stark.
Since Trump's insurrection, less than two weeks
have passed; we're glad democracy survived
rebellion and the awfulest of Tweets –
there was no Civil War, and we're alive!
Joe Biden's such a change from that, indeed:
for unity he stresses his concern.
At last, a President who'll truly lead!
I hope from these four years there's much we've learned.
Kamala Harris already so much has meant,
a Woman of Color is our Vice President!

Orion
1-21-21

Thou, recognizable constellation
so large, glowing in the winter night sky,
in earliest mythic stories mentioned art.
Orion! With thy belt and dangling sword,
a figure most imposing to the eye,
you stand up tall when summer says goodbye.
Traditions naming thee must ancient be,
for once remembered, who'd forget thy name?
The hunter! Archètype so masculine,
those first-named stars a star did represent:
to people long ago a folk hero,
the mighty hunter men aspired to be.

Likely predating the Olympian gods,
the later storytellers him despised,
provincial and barbaric Orion;
thus stories they invented about him:
disgusting origin and deeds most fell,
the hero's downfall and his just disgrace.

Yet later centuries, the poets great
his myth revived, and gave a brand-new spin
to stories of Orion the Hunter.

Wise Istros, lover, poet, satirist,
imagined Artemis falling in love
with that great hunter who her talents matched.
Her jealous brother, Apollo the god,
did trick her into shooting her lover:
she thought it target practice, loosed the shaft.
As lightning from the hand of Zeus it sped
so swiftly that it struck him in the head.
To shore his corse it drifted, and she shrieked
in horror when she saw what she had done.

But Ovid to the Scorpion's deadly sting
attributes violent death and sky placement:
our hero leapt bravely to the defense
of Leto, and he was stung in her stead –
tho 'twas his fault, in fact, for Gaea sent
his murd'rer to protect the creatures wild
from his excessive zeal – he'd kill them all!
An early indication this may be
that hunting out of season was taboo.
The management of wildlife is a trust,
and we must be responsible, and think
so all the creatures wild might thrive and grow
and we might live as one with Mother Earth.

Sowing Day
1-23-21

A Sowing Day the Romans did proclaim
upon that season's day when seed was sown,
the land receptive to the farming rites.
Bright garlands hung in wreaths on oxen strong
and ye may rest who've tilled and sown the earth.
A holiday did farmers celebrate
and stroll from house to house with joy to share.
They to their neighbors gave the cakes of spelt
in honor of Ceres, goddess of grain;
and to her, cattle sacrifice was made.
May fragile sprouts to seedlings strong well grow
may fields untroubled by cold late snow be
May gentle rains and warming sun give grace,
may birds and herds stay clear of fresh-tilled fields
May golden grains grow strong, from mildew free,
not withering, and neither over-bold.
May fields be free of weeds, may crops grow tall

May Earth be fertile and reward thy work
May warriors to ploughshares beat their swords,
and mattocks make in place of javelins.
May we our efforts turn to harmony
and nurture Peace, O Ceres, nurture Peace,
as we nurture the Peace that nurtures thee.

Gratitude, Not Bitterness
1-24-21

Let gratitude, not bitterness,
        be the focus of my mind:
appreciation, thankfulness,
        and trying to be kind.

For blessings down upon me rain,
        beauty before my eyes:
when I can look around again,
        these things I realize.

So gratitude, not bitterness,
        shall all my focus be:
appreciation, thankfulness,
        recurring thoughts for me.

Our Leaders Are Not Gods
1-27-21.ii

In his poem 'bout the brothers Geminid,
Ovid describes the Emperors as 'gods.'
Back in the day, that's what the people did,
for any who defied them faced long odds
as our poèt himself did so well know:
he surely reservations had – meanwhile
he made grand statements loyalty to show,
and lived out his remaining days exiled.
A stately headdress, ceremonial robes
surely can make a Pharaoh look quite grand;
but godliness is not conferred by clothes
or titles – don't let things get out of hand.
Let us never get to that point again.
Our leaders are not gods: they are human!

Perhaps Rashly
1-28-21

Grey are the clouds in the January sky
and the plants ev'rywhere are winter-brown,
tho I know not whether to expect rain.
Among the world's most fortunate people,
I'm privileged to be living where I do,
in this our house, outside town, near a creek,
with wife most beautiful and two great kids.
We should to creekside walk each Helios ride,
tho weather and circumstance complicate
and make our creekside walks more special days.

In carrying out a resolution
undertaken on the spur of the moment
I have, perhaps rashly, filled half of this,
the second handwritten notebook volume
of my *Annum Poetica* project,
with musings long, and angry words, and dreams,
more fodder for endless critics to burn:
such folks would sneer even at Hannibal
who marched his elephants across the pass
of snowy Alps, and took the fight to Rome.
Th' opinions of such as they matter not.

It's been nearly a year since quarantine
Corona Virus to contain began
and I've been trying to homeschool my kids
all this time, while my essential wife works.
The world has changed greatly in the meantime,
but we remain the same deep in our hearts.
We are but human, flawed and passionate,
by our emotions driven, despite claims
of rational behavior well thought-out.

February, 2021

75 Hard Begins
2-1-21

Perhaps it seems a strange thing for a bard –
today I begin "75 Hard,"
a mental toughness and fitness program.
I'm hopeful this will help change who I am:
a structured routine my life to revamp,
myself through paces put, like a boot camp!

I plan my life to change in many ways,
jump-start with the next 75 days.
And when I reach the end, I'll give a shout,
thus my poetic year I shall close out.

Immolc
2-2-21

This holiday repurposed many times
has been, throughout the years, and new names giv'n.
It always celebrates the way sun shines
a little brighter in these days we're livin'.
Midway between Solstice and Equinox,
the Pagans named it Imbolc, when the ewes
began to birth new lambs, replenish stocks,
we celebrate the life that now ensues.
The Cath'lics, Pagan holiday then tamed,
but still they celebrated Sun's return
when Candlemas this day they did rename
and blessed the candles which through winter burned.
America made it sillièr still
with Groundhog Day, and Punxsutawney Phil!

Life's Strange Looking-Glass
2-3-21

Although on projects I'm falling behind,
at least I don't feel I'm losing my mind.
I surely have felt that way in the past,
such as last summer; but it did not last.
The lightning storm has cleared up in my head;
on other things I can focus instead.
It's true, sometimes I still have thoughts I hate,
but I'm less likely to persevorate.
I don't think this was due to any trick:
when neurons misfire, my brain is a dick!
It took some time and calm for it to pass.
Now I reflect on life's strange looking-glass,
consider what future will make me glad
as husband, writer, musician, and Dad.

On Top
2-7-21

You know, sometimes
    when things get rough
Ya gotta look deep inside
    remember you're enough

And sometimes
    you need a little blessing
There is no shame
    there is no shame in asking

It's okay to take some time
    when you hit that wall
we all need a bit of help sometimes
    it's not the Fall

And ev'ry step
    brings you closer to your goal
so keep tryin' when things get hard
    next thing you know

You're gonna come out right on top
    with the world
In the palm of your hand

We all have tried
    and sometimes we all have failed, too
Don't take it so hard
    have faith that it's not just you

Pick yourself back up
    and set your feet back on the path walkin'
Call up a loved one
    set your mind free when you do some talkin'

So baby take some time
    one and all
We're just feelin' a little helplessness
    it's not the Fall

And ev'ry step
    brings us closer to the goal
So keep tryin' when things get hard
    next thing you know

You're gonna come out right on top
    of the world
In the palm of your hand

You can do it!
    Better late than never
Put your mind into it
    Nothing lasts forever

So ev'rybody take some time
    one and all
We're just feelin' a little helplessness
    it's not the Fall
And ev'ry step
    brings us closer to the goal
So keep tryin' when things get hard
    next thing you know

You're gonna come out right on top
    with the world
In the palm of your hand

The Power of Affirmation
2-8-21

An affirmation power has, I'm told,
our attitudes and thoughts to shape and guide.
Could this help me to combat patterns old,
and negativity I keep inside?
Perhaps 'twill help me to gain some control
over perpetual darkling spiral down –
envisioning fulfillment of a goal
could really help to turn one's life around?
I'm told to state it in the present tense
and squelch that nagging voice that screams out, "Lie!"
Believing it could happen makes some sense;
embodying my goals is worth a try.
Affirming vision's hope perhaps I'll find
that confidence is just a state of mind.

A Visualization
2-8-21.ii

I am a writer, and I've always been.
I am a musician, since way back when.
I've been an entrepreneur now for decades.
People love my work, it wins accolades.
My books are read by people I don't know.
My songs are playing on the radio.
And for my business work, folks give me thanks!
I have a fortune saved up in the bank.
I had to hire a slew of employees
to keep up with new customers saying, "Please!"
I have paid off all of my family's debts.
I've made an impact folks will ne'er forget.

My Internal Judge Criticizes My Visualization
2-8-21.iii

I write these words while sitting on the couch,
so far from them, my brain is screaming, "Ouch!"
Perhaps if these goals I can make myself say,
these affirmations of mine will be true someday.

The Second Impeachment
2-9-21

Trump never cared about democracy,
'twas clear from the beginning of his term.
Rejecting mass appeal and compromise,
he rallied up his hater base with hate
'gainst immigrants, and racial groups, and truth,
and women, and decency, and the law.
When four years later Trump th' election lost,
refused he to accept the results true
and spent two months spewing his baseless lies
because he did not care 'bout what was right
but only wanted power to retain.
Attempted he rebellion to incite!

For hours it seemed that he succeeded had.
The haters stormed the Congress in their rage,
intent on murdering the leaders true.
Had they succeeded in their violent goals,
there's no doubt that they surely would have killed
Pelosi, AOC, and even Pence;
and ev'ryone with whom they disagreed.
And as it was, two policemen they killed:
those haters who claim to support police
were screaming "Fuck the blue!" and "Traitor pigs!" –
assaulted they police with a flag pole.
The angry mob was chanting, "Stop the steal!"
by which they meant, "End this democracy!"
No reas'nable person really believes
the lies that Trump repeats about the vote.
A lie repeated oft is still a lie.
And Trump intended that his lies would send
his angry mob the Congress to attack.

It was intentional. He watched with glee
events unfolding on television
in hopes at last he could seize total pow'r.
At last he learned it would not be enough:
advisors who had better sense than he
convinced him, ask the mob depart from hence.
Remorse showed he none, regret not at all:
continued he instead his baseless lies,
attacks upon our grand democracy.

Today the Senate has Trump's trial commenced,
the second time that he has been impeached.
Impeachment managers showed video,
a montage of the violent mob that day.
A most disturbing sight it was to see:
that viōlent attempt to overthrow
this democratic government of ours
and to supplant it with dictatorship
for Donald Trump's authoritarian rule.
But we all know, before this even starts,
the Senate trial will Trump "not guilty" find,
because the Senators are chickenshit
and fear that Trump's mad mob will take revenge
if they should dare to stand up for what's right.
They're joined in unity by naked fear.
There is no hope for justice in this case,
no consequences Trump shall ever face
despite his open acts of treason high.
Acquitted Trump will be, to lasting shame.
There is no justice, no justice at all.

I ask you now: if we cannot convict
that traitor Donald Trump, who did incite
rebellion 'gainst these, our United States:
what business have we ever to convict
anyone of anything, ever again?
The Justice system is badly broken:

the innocent condemned, guilty let free.
The very concept of "justice" is fraud.
There is no justice, no justice at all.

The Ice Storm
2-12-21.ii

I sit here on my couch and write
by flick'ring flames of candlelight.
Always I hope for some insight
while journeying into the night.

Likely this day we'll not forget,
of this winter the coldest yet.
We find that in our ways we're set
when normal life is a safe bet.

But last night hard the rain did freeze
upon the branches of the trees
which break and crumble in the breeze
and bring civilization to its knees

when power lines the branches sever –
that's why this night's the coldest ever.
We people think we're oh, so clever.
Are we prepared for this? No, never!

We narrow down what we require
and huddle we around the fire
as cold night does our hearts inspire
to speak of what we most desire.

Zappy Zout
2-12-21.iv

Zippy zappy zout,
the power is still out
that's what this poem's about
my belly is too stout
I shall not scream and shout
I have no social clout
I'm always filled with doubt
but my talents I tout
avoid a fighting bout
no matter who calls me "lout"
so zippy, zappy, zout
the power is still out!

The Ice Storm's Aftermath
2-13-21

Huge trees are broken,
  power lines down
we had to drive over them
  to get in to town

There's no running water
  no electricity
Not even cell phone service
  it's a strange place to be

Just to flush the toilets
  I hauled water from the flooded creek
Our second natural disaster in six months
  it's not a lifestyle for the weak!

Our lives have been disrupted
      by this huge ice storm
We'll be all right, I'm certain,
        but this is not the norm!

Downed Power Lines
2-14-21.iv

There were downed power lines across the road,
and lanes were blocked by the trees fallen down.
Was it courage or foolishness we showed
when we drove over them to get to town?
This ice storm helps us remember the hours
that we are sometimes likely to forget
as we for sev'ral days live without power:
no central heat, no phones, no Internet.
Although without a stove it's hard to cook,
nor running water to wash e'en one dish;
the trees are broken, far as one might look,
I could the branches clear, long as I wished;
we are so fortunate, to help us pass
this time, our generator runs on gas.

To Essential Workers
2-15-21

You were there for us when there was no electricity
Though lines were long, you helped us cheerfully
You were there for us in our time of need
We are so grateful to you, indeed
If we may, we would like to say this, please:
Thank you, you're heroes, store employees!

Do Not Trust the Winds
2-15-21.ii

Today a warning Ovid has for us:
do not trust the winds, this time of year!
As if he needs to tell me, who has been
out through the day, fall'n branches to clear!

President's Day (Observed)
2.15.21.v

Today is President's Day Observed,
it's usually a bank holiday;
but with the ice storms, it's a bit absurd
to keep talking; what can I say?
      I sit and watch the fire burn.
      Some day I shall return
to Washington and Lincoln's tales convey.

75 Hard Continues
2-16-21.iii

My Lent ritual I early began.
Among other men, I am just a man.
Although perhaps uncommon for a bard,
I persevere at "75 Hard"
despite the power outages and ice,
I have not given in – though it'd be nice!
     I'm sticking with the program
     and changing who I am:
no alcohol; and two workouts a day,
each 45 minutes, and one outside.
Just a couple more things before I play,
just a couple more things before I ride:
a daily shirtless selfie, please don't shriek;
a gallon of water (gotta take a leak);
     pick a diet and stick to it,
     that's the only way to do it;
and read ten pages of a self-help book,
changing how I think, not just how I look.

Writing By Candlelight
2-18-21

Again I write by candlelight
and sit before the fire at night.
It crumbles our society
when we have no 'lectricity.
By flick'ring light it's hard to see,
and people keep talking to me.
I guess it's time to get off my ass
and pour the generator more gas.

A Terrible Smell
2-19-21

The kitchen's filled with a terrible smell
when I open the fridge: "What's this fresh Hell?"
The food in my fridge is going bad,
I threw away much of what we had.
We've gone a week now without power
living day by day, hour by hour.
But Texas this week has had it worse:
yes, Climate Change is a modern curse!

Creek Water
2-20-21

I boil water from the creek
  to wash dishes,
I haul water from the creek
  to flush the toilets.
We've been without power for a week;
  I'm making wishes.
Thank the gods we live near a creek
  so I can boil it!

In Memoriam
2-20-21.ii

This morning while scrolling my social feed, I
upon a post I'd not expected came –
it notified the local Pagan folk
a man who we all knew just killed himself;
no explanation offered, or required.
I wish he could have seen all the replies,
the outpouring of grief and memories.
Perhaps if he'd have known how we all felt
he'd still be smiling and alive today.
The loneliness and dark nights visit all,
but please remember that it does not last:
eventually the sunshine will return.

Rise Above
2-21-21.ii

Sometimes we get too down on ourselves.
We spiral where the darkness dwells;
and many pieces have to move
before things will start to improve.

But there is always hope when you look,
from other people, or a self-help book;
and in time, we can finally rise above
and begin to dwell in a place of love.

Leaping to Judgment
2-22-21.iv : Inspired by Dante, *Paradiso*, Canto XIII lines 112-140

Thy feet thou shouldst move slowly
      like as though they were filled with lead
rather than leap to judgments
      and let assumptions fill thy head.

Too often we most thoughtlessly
      do cry out "Yes!" or "No!"
but when we fail to give matters thought
      we are brought down quite low.

When we quickly to judgment leap,
      often false is our choice.
Then, rather than admit we've made a mistake
      we'll defend it with our last voice.

For we're too full of confidence
      when arrogant vanity assumes –
the intellect admits no wrong,
      such errors lead to doom!

Shouldst thou go seeking for the truth
      yet not apply rational thought,
then thou art like to ne'er return –
      so recall what you were taught.

Think of the brambles in winter-time
      that look like dry dead vines
yet burst forth into floral blooms
      when on them summer sun shines.

Reck not the harvest afore it's ripe
      nor chickens before they hatch,
and guess not which of thy neighbors sins most:
      for there are limits to thy watch!

A Civil Obligation
2-23-21

Tomorrow I have jury duty:
"Get downtown, and shake your booty!
  You don't want to? Well, you'd best
  or else you'll be under arrest!"

Five Hundred Thousand Dead
2-23-21.ii

The problem of disinformation
is a key challenge facing our nation.
It has contributed to the Corona Virus spread,
and now there are half a million dead
just here in these United States.
A half a million is a loss so great –
if we could have saved them, why hesitate?
But the rise of vicious anti-maskers
has turned this into a fucking disaster.
It's all because Trump did insist
he's always been on top of it,
as a way for him to duty shirk
instead of putting in the real hard work!
His version of reality
is all his supporters want to see.
Now patients in hospitals, nearing death,
are screaming out with their very last breath,
"It's just a hoax! Covid's not real!"
But the virus cares not how you feel.
We'll conquer it, with any luck;
but until then, wear a mask, you dumb fuck!

Jury Duty
2-24-21

Getting to the courthouse
        involved so much shit
I was kind of looking forward
        to voting to acquit

although I know nothing of the case
and never saw the defendant's face –
you've read the words I have spoken:
I believe the justice system's broken!

The prosecution would have had
        to work hard to convince me
not to vote to let
        the defendant go free.

Somehow they looked at me
        and they knew,
and said, "Thanks, but no.
        Get out of here, you!"

A Dash of "What the Hell"
2-25-21

With a little bit of "fuck it"
     and a dash of "what the Hell"
I set my feet on a new path,
     left the one they knew so well.

With a little bit of "You got this"
     I decided to make that change,
Ignoring all the naysayers
     who said I was deranged.

Believing I could make that change
     I chose to take a new route;
And now at last I can enjoy
     my labor's well-earned fruit!

March, 2021

March's Namesake
3-1-21

It's war! The month of Mars doth celebrate
the conflict central to our human lives –
for we must stand our ground, not hesitate
goals to pursue, *take* that for which we strive.
The songbirds have returned, in trees they sing,
the clouds are fluffy in blue morning sky.
Although we know not what tomorrow brings
the sunny days encourage us to try.
This is the month of which folks long have said,
"Comes in like a lion, out like a lamb"
but I just want to control my own head
with thoughts focused on who I think I am.
I'll fight to my identity define,
and soldier on until I take what's mine!

Each One
3-2-21

Each one of us has seen
      through years what we have seen.
That's why we each believe
      what each of us believes.
And through our lives we try
      to do what seems to us right.
The past shapes our sense of self
      and the values for which we fight.

"Personality Isn't Permanent"
3-3-21

All of us are changing, ev'ry day;
    sometimes for better, sometimes for worse.
It shows in what we think and what we say,
    it affects the life story that we rehearse.
Now it's become a rebellious act just to suggest
    there's anything flexible about identity,
but that's a thought we must embrace to be our best:
    we really can decide who we want to be.
The haters scream out, "No! You are who you are,
    and the worst moment of your life is the real you!"
We've got to say "Fuck those guys" if we want to go far
    and let our higher aspirations shine on through.

Time Management
3-9-21

I may have overcommitted
and then I "Oh, shit" - ed!
I'll tell you the major facts:
it's the week to file business tax.
I am always behind
feel like I'm losing my mind
but the real problem's how my time's spent:
it's a matter of management.

A Year Outside of Time
3-11-21

One year ago today
 the pandemic was declared.
We knew not what would happen,
 but we were feeling pretty scared:
facing such a great unknown
 there was no way to be prepared.

It's been nearly a year
 since the lockdown began
with the virus – and the fear –
 sweeping 'cross the land
but denial from the White House
 let it get out of hand.

And yes, some might argue
 that it could have been worse;
but the novel Corona Virus
 has surely been a curse,
and so many deaths could have been prevented
 if we'd all taken it seriously from the first.

There have not been any zombies
 and the world did not quite end,
but more than half a million Americans
 the virus to early graves did send.
This has not been easy for us
 no, we cannot pretend –

And for some it's been much harder,
 so many their jobs have lost,
but rather than provide support
 Congress whined about the cost;
and without a safety net in place,
 many out on the streets were tossed.

By the virus and the lockdown
     this year has been defined.
Cooped up in isolation,
     the whole world lost its mind!
We fell apart in stasis,
     a year outside of time.

The Springtime Month
3-12-21

Time was, the year began with March – in Rome
the early calendar had a blank space
for those most cold and bleak of winter months;
those two which now begin our ev'ry year
were not worth marking out, so long ago!
But March! Although the Springtime's not begun
according to the Equinoctial date,
try telling that to birds nesting in trees,
try telling that to daffodils in bloom,
try telling that to Earth so vivid green
try telling that to warm sun and blue skies.
We see the ducks a-swimming in the creek,
a silly woodpecker pecked on our house,
the ants are back to crawling through the walls,
the floodwaters recede, and joy returns.

O March! Our praise to thee, the springtime month,
a time of change when all the world's renewed,
and there is nothing more we need right now
so bless us with renewing change and joy
that we may be renewed, body and soul.
No wonder 'tis, when Romulus of myth
first calendar made, it began with March:
foundation of the year when all things change.

Daylight Savings Time
3-14-21

No time is saved by clock change trickery,
but it's a habit for society.
Although the benefits are hard to see,
from Daylight Savings Time we'll ne'er be free!

Fat Guitar Tone
3-16-21

Give me that fat tone, with the booming bass,
the ballsy mids fill out the punchy sound,
and just enough high end to make it shine.
Too often the sound's nothing but treble,
it sounds tinny and dull, flat and lifeless,
a deadpan transistor without a soul.
No, no more, get that shit away from me!
I'm switching my guitar to heavier strings,
a tube amp for a warm distortion sound,
and overdrive pedals for my high gain!

Labels Ain't My Bag
3-16-21.ii

Take that label off me
        I don't want a tag
I just want to be free
        labels ain't my bag.

A lot of people think
        that it's really great
when all the options shrink –
        but that just leads to hate!

As long as we identify
        with those labels we choose
we never are inclined to try
        to challenge words we use.

And then we mock the other side
        for being "sensitive,"
accusing them of tryin' to hide –
        but *we* have no fucks to give...

Until they treat us the same way:
        we find the tables turned;
we wish they would watch what they say,
        for now we feel quite burned!

Too often we label sisters and brothers
        and we think it is just fine;
but then when we are labeled by others
        they tell us, "Don't you whine!"

It's only when we find we've been
     labeled by enemies,
we tend to reprimand them then –
     "No, don't talk like that, please!"

Yes, sticks and stones may break my bones
     but words may hurt me worse;
for wounds heal when I'm left alone,
     but confidence destroyed is hard to reverse.

Ostara
3-20-21

The day and night are of an equal length
today – it is the day that Spring begins!
Ostara is the Vernal Equinox
and tho it rains, the sunshine's close at hand:
it spreads its warmth and joy across the land.
The flowers bloom! The yellow daffodils
with bells that open like a choir to sing
their praises to the glory of the sky
and give their thanks for ev'ry passing day,
this wond'rous chance to be alive on Earth
surrounded by the green of growing things
that sprout and grow with vibrance and with strength
as life returns to all the land in Spring.
So be like as the daffodils, and praise
this opportunity to be alive.
We give thanks to the Sun, and to the rain,
we bless the Moon and stars up in the sky,
we bless the flowers as they bloom and grow;
we wish that same prosperity and growth
will bless all of our lives throughout the year.

Being My Best Self
3-22-21

I'm setting myself deadlines
trying to take control of my time
to overcome my uncertain mind
I'm setting myself deadlines.

I'm writing out my long-term goals
I know they will be good for my soul
gonna turn my mental shit into gold
by writing out my long-term goals.

I'm planning how my life will change
tho some people might think it strange
if I want it to rearrange
I must plan how my life will change

I'm trying to learn not to care
that haters point and scream "Beware!"
to keep me isolated where
I am, that's why I must not care.

I want to learn to be my best,
it matters not who is impressed.
I do not like to be distressed,
so I must learn to be my best.

An Integrated Man
3-24-21

If I live my life according to plan,
will that help me be an integrated man?
If I schedule out my days, dawn to night,
will my activities soon cease to excite?

If I plan my life based on my goals,
will that bring fulfillment to my soul?
I will not know unless I try
to achieve great things before I die!

Palm Sunday
3-28-21

Events like this are rare within one's life:
to be so wildly welcomed by the crowds
they line the avenues with fronds of palm
and cheer to watch you pass on down the street,
a borrowed burro serving as your mount.
It is a glory time, so savor it:
success like this presages certain fall,
as those with powèr turn envy on you
and they begin to plot your certain doom.

Recall how Jesus joined Jerusalem:
the throngs of crowds all welcomed his approach,
but just five days had passed when all that changed
and those same crowds all cheered his tortured death,
for popular opinion does not last:
both cheers and insults fade into the past.

Another Rabbit
3-29-21

This morning I saw a rabbit again –
a smaller one than last year's friend
who came to an untimely end.
Best wishes to this new one I send!

Conspiracy Theories
3-30-21

I got a phone call from an old friend last night.
It soon became clear all was not quite right...
It seemed that ev'ry word out of his mouth
was a conspiracy theory he did espouse.
These past few years, as the world was going to hell,
down the QAnon rabbit hole he fell.
I just felt sad, rather than enraged
when he claimed mass shootings were "false flag staged."
When he said, "*plan*demic" I shook my head
at how easily he dismissed half a million dead.[1]
But I really felt that I was being taken for a ride
when he popped out with the term, "White genocide."
Where did my old friend's thinking go so wrong?
With him I once wrote "The Bipolar Song."
When drunk and unemployed, we tend t'wards views extreme:
instead of learning to become serene,
we fill our minds with bullshit memes.

---

1   We're now at 550,000 according to this morning's news report.

Luna
3-31-21

O great and glorious Moon
    you rule the night
and when you wax to full
    you shine so bright.

They say you tug the seas
    and raise the tides
which helped free that cargo ship from the Suez Canal –
    it was stuck in wide!

To thee all lonely lovers look
    and raise their eyes
"O Moon please bring me my love,"
    they sadly cry.

In Rome, thousands of years ago,
    on this very night
the people walked atop the Aventine Ridge
    for a sacred rite.

Luna the Moon they worshiped
    there in the open air,
with praises and glorious song,
    with love and care.

April, 2021

Mental Toughness
4-2-21.ii

The opinions of other folks
    I must disregard.
Whether they are good or bad,
    make my mind hard.

Yes, other folks talk loads of shit –
    it matters not!
On all that is good in my life
    I'll focus my thoughts.

Visiting Family for Easter
4-3-21

This year has been so wrong
for we have gone so long
without seeing each other:
brother, sister, father, mother.
We've spent so much time inside
while so many have died.
The world turned upside-down –
reverberations resound
through each and ev'ry brain
with such sadness and pain.
The homeless population
has increased across the nation.
Small businesses collapsed
as social norms have lapsed.
With the vaccine there's hope for normality,
and at last, we're able to see family!

We Each Must Choose
4-7-21

To chance, our lives we cannot leave
if we our goals wish to achieve.
A conscious path we each must choose
if we our goals wish to pursue.
Envision ourselves at the heights we'll soar
if from our lives we wish for more.
Then write we out a detailed plan,
if we wish to do the best we can.

Spring Cleaning
4-10-21.ii

Today we did Spring cleaning,
        the attic and the shop.
We swept and rearranged
        until we had to stop.
We built a big bonfire
        right there in our driveway,
we burned up downed branches and trash
        until the end of the day.
Then my wife got us all pizza
        as a dinner treat,
and we watched an ev'ning movie:
        "Hercules" was really neat.

...

Between Extremes
4-12-21

"The summer is too hot,
  the winter is too cold.
  First you are too young,
  and then you are too old."

When nothing will suffice,
perhaps it would be nice,
rather than wish away,
to just enjoy today.

75 Days Later
4-17-21.ii

Can you believe it's been seventy-five
long days since I began the challenge hard?
I am so fortunate to be alive,
regardless of my talents as a bard.
I can report that I'm both pleased and shocked,
for me, this was quite a tremendous win:
full twenty-two pounds in this time I have dropped –
it's been two decades since I was this thin!
By social media haters called deranged,
by toxic friends from my past written off.
I made a choice, and my life I have changed!
Yes, now it's on, no matter how they scoff.
And I will never stop until I've won:
with this round over, my fight's just begun!

A Verdict
4-20-21.iii

This has been going on for quite a while:
the officer who killed George Floyd's on trial.
At last the verdict for which we had prayed:
that murderer was found guilty today.
It was captured on video: we saw!
And nobody should be above the law.
You've seen the thoughts these pages have contained –
for lack of justice I often complained.
As April's sun shines down with loving rays,
the world is filled with hope for brand-new days.

Gratitude to a Mentor
4-21-21.ii

As time's gone on, sweet Ovid, I've relied
more heavily upon thy poems for mine,
rather than inspiration from inside,
or showered down from the spirits divine.
I thank thee, poet: tales of thy exile
provided me with company throughout
the lonely months that for me were a trial:
I felt you knew what I was sad about.
And now, from my own *Tristia* I've returned!
I have admired your view of history.
I think back on the lessons I have learned
from pondering your ancient poetry.
Your thoughtful words allowed your thoughts to spread,
although two thousand years you have been dead!

The Rites of the Shepherds
4-21-21.iii

This day the Romans celebrate the shepherd's rites
with ashes from cow fetus sacrifice,
the beanstalks and burnt offerings in hand.
Then three times over candles they would leap
and sprinkle water from their laurel wands:
perhaps the origin of witchcraft tales!
There are more details, they're set forth within
the poems of Ovid, read them if you dare,
ye scholars, lovers, poets, and weirdos,
read his fucking poems, you know you want to!

An Auspicious Conclusion
4-21-21.iv

Blue are the skies, the sunny Springtime skies,
without a cloud, no, not one hint of rain.
I have been reading Ovid's *Fasti* poems,
and poet's inspiration I pursued.

A year and a day I have scribbled lines.
By hand two artsy notebooks I have filled
with poems 'bout calendars, heroes, and gods,
events of great moment, and my life, too.
This year has been historic, none can doubt:
Corona Virus lockdowns changed our lives,
the Black Lives Matter protests changed our hearts,
the Trump-led insurrection showed our hate.

My two young sons are still in school from home.
Despite conditions, they have persevered.
Tho suited for the task I'll never be,
it has grown easier as time has passed.
My loving wife's essential to us all,
hard-working, she vaccine administers
to try to bring about pandemic's end.

This year has changed the world, we all have changed,
tho dubious the lessons we have learned –
on one another we have turned online,
divides as deep as ever they have been,
and compromise anathema to all.

Today is quite auspicious to complete
this year of poetry, and I thank you
dear reader, you have joined in this journey,
and what a whirlwind year this one has been,
as we adventured 'round the Sun once more!
I hope these thoughts on calendars have shown
how much we have in common across time.

Now go in peace, dear reader, spread the love,
teach one another to be tolerant;
but for injustice, give no quarter, none –
not even when it comes from your own side!
Remember always, please, that life can change:
our personality and circumstance.
No matter if you're stuck, or in exile,
you can contentment find, there's always hope;
never forget that there is always hope.

finis

Afterword

What a year that was!

The time period covered by this collection of poems (April 2020 to April 2021) included the Covid-19 pandemic lockdowns; the Black Lives Matter protests sparked by the murder of George Floyd by a police officer; the deadly wildfires that burned the West; the Presidential election of 2020; the January 6 insurrection by right-wing rioters who violently stormed the Capitol building; and the winter ice storms that knocked out our electricity and plunged us into darkness.

Just two months after this collection's conclusion, there was yet another natural disaster. Beginning in late June of 2021, a massive heat wave set temperature records across the American West for almost a week. The heat wave exacerbated drought conditions, devastated plants and crops, and caused hundreds of deaths. Although that experience is not included within this collection, it has certainly contributed to a growing apocalyptic sensibility in modern culture.

During my year of poetry, I wrote nearly 700 poems.

By necessity, the present volume omits the majority of those pieces. Simply put, few readers have the time!

The best pieces will be published in carefully curated volumes, each with its own subject and focus:

Choosing Change, a selection of poems about mindset and personal transformation.

Months and Days, a selection of poems about the modern calendar, along with various holidays and cultural and religious celebrations and observances.

The Histories, a selection of poems about historical figures and events.

Poems for the Holidays, a short selection of poems focused solely on the Yule holiday season.

A Different Thousand and One Nights, an expanded collection of poems retelling popular fairy tales, myths, and legends.

And the present volume, *A Year Outside of Time*, a collection of poems sharing a personal perspective on the historic events of 2020 and early 2021.

If you have enjoyed these poems, I hope you will consider reading one of those other volumes as well.

Thank you for joining me on this journey, dear reader. Wishing you grace, dignity, and compassion, today and every day.

Titus Naso

References and Resources

The "75 Hard" Mental Toughness Program was created and promoted by Andy Frisella. You can learn more about the program from the following links:

Overview: "75 Hard | The 75-Day Tactical Guide to Winning the War with Yourself"
https://andyfrisella.com/pages/75hard-info

Podcast: "75HARD: A 75-Day Tactical Guide to Winning the War With Yourself, with Andy Frisella - MFCEO290"
https://andyfrisella.com/blogs/mfceo-project-podcast/75hard-a-75-day-tactical-guide-to-winning-the-war-with-yourself-with-andy-frisella-mfceo291

Book: "75 Hard: A Tactical Guide to Winning the War with Yourself" by Andy Frisella.
https://andyfrisella.com/products/75-hard-a-tactical-guide-to-winning-the-war-with-yourself

I referenced a number of Wikipedia entries through the year. I have not cited all of these articles individually, but I thank Wikipedia as an invaluable resource to the layperson who wishes to pursue a variety of interests.

I gratefully referenced the following resources:

Abrams, M.H., et al., editors. (1993 ed.) *The Norton Anthology of English Literature: Sixth Edition, Volume 1*. New York, NY: W. W. Norton & Company

Alighieri, Dante. (1952 ed.). *The Divine Comedy of Dante Alighieri: Tranlated by Charles Eliot Norton*. Great Books of the Western World vol. 21: Dante. Chicago, IL: The University of Chicago Press (Encyclopædia Britannica, Inc.)

Allighieri, Dante: *Paradise*. (2006 ed). Read by Heathcote Williams. Naxos AudioBooks via Libby.

Allighieri, Dante. (2006 ed.) *Purgatory from the Divine Comedy: read by Heathcote Williams*. Audiobook. Naxos AudioBooks via Libby.

Amen, Daniel G. (2008 ed.) *Change Your Brain, Change Your Life*. Narrated by the author. Audiobook. Random House Audio via Libby.

Angelou, Maya. (2006). *Celebrations: Rituals of Peace and Prayer, Read by the Author. An Unabridged Production*. Audiobook. Random House Audio via Libby.

Angus, David. (2006 ed.). *Moses*. Audiobook. Read by Kerry Shale. Audiobook. Naxos Audiobooks via Libby.

Aurelius, Marcus (Maxwell Staniforth, trans. & introd.) (1964 ed.) *Meditations*. New York, NY: Penguin Books USA Inc. (Penguin Classics).

Bede. (trans, ed, intro, notes & commentary by Faith Wallis). (2012 ed). *Bede: The Reckoning of Time, Translated with introduction, notes and commentary by Faith Wallis*. Translated Texts for Historians, Volume 29. Liverpool, UK: Liverpool University Press.

Ben-Shahar, Tal. (2007). *Happier: Learn the Secrets to Daily Joy and Lasting Fulfillment*. San Francisco, CA: McGraw-Hill.

Blake, William. (2005 ed.). *William Blake: Selected Poems*. Read by Frederick Davidson. Audiobook. Blackstone Audio, Inc. and Buck 50 Productions, LLC via Libby.

Brown, Brené. (2015 ed.) *Rising Strong: How the Ability to Reset Transforms the Way We Live, Love, Parent, and Lead. Read by the Author | Unabridged.* Audiobook. Random House Audio via Libby.

Catullus. (trans. Guy Lee). (1998 ed.) *The Poems of Catullus: Edited and translated with an Introduction and Notes by Guy Lee.* Oxford, UK: Oxford University Press (Oxford World's Classics).

Chaucer, Geoffrey. (trans. David Wright). (1988 ed.) *The Canterbury Tales: A verse translation with an Introduction and Notes by David Wright.* Aylesbury, Bucks: Oxford University Press (The World's Classics).

Chaucer, Geoffrey. *The Canterbury Tales: Volume II.* (2005 ed). Read by Philip Madoc, Frances Jeater, John Rowe, Charles Simpson and John Moffatt. Naxos AudioBooks via Libby.

Chaucer, Geoffrey. (1952 ed.) *Troilus and Cressida and The Canterbury Tales by Geoffrey Chaucer: with modern English versions of both works.* Great Books of the Western World vol. 22: Chaucer. Chicago, IL: The University of Chicago Press (Encyclopædia Britannica, Inc.)

Cohen, Marshall. (July 9, 2020). *'Broken heart syndrome' has increased during the Covid-19 pandemic, small study suggests.* CNN. https://www.cnn.com/2020/07/09/health/broken-heart-syndrome-coronavirus-wellness/index.html

de Grasse Tyson, Neil. (2017). *Astrophysics for People in a Hurry: Read by the Author | Unabridged.* Audiobook. Blackstone Publishing via Libby.

Doyle, Arthur Conan. (2009 ed.). *The Adventures of Sherlock Holmes.* Narrated by Ralph Cosham. Audiobook. Blackstone Publishing via Libby.

Dickinson, Emily. (Christanne Miller, ed.). (2016). *Emily Dickinson's Poems As She Preserved Them.* Cambridge, MA: The Belknap Press of Harvard University Press.

Division of Christian Education of the National Council of the Churches of Christ in the United States of America. (1959). *The Holy*

Bible: Revised Standard Version containing the Old and New Testaments, Translated from the Original Tongues. Camden, NJ: Thomas Nelson Inc.

Dodge, Theodore Ayrault. (orig. 1889, 2005 ed.) *Hannibal: Introduction by Ian M. Cuthbertson.* New York, NY: Barnes & Noble, Inc.

Eratosthenes and Hyginus. (Robin Hard, trans., introd. & notes). (2015). *Constellation Myths with Aratus's Phaenomena.* Oxford, UK: Oxford University Press (Oxford World's Classics).

Epicurus (George K. Strodach, trans. & introd., foreword by Daniel Klein). (2012 ed.) *The Art of Happiness.* New York, NY: Penguin Books (Penguin Group USA, Inc.)

Frankl, Victor E. (2004 ed.) *Man's Search for Meaning.* Narrated by Simon Vance. Audiobook. Blackstone Audio, Inc. and Buck 50 Productions, LLC via Libby.

(Unknown). Flynn, Benedict, trans. *Sir Gawain and the Green Knight: New verse translation by Benedict Flynn.* (2008 ed.) Read by Jasper Britton. Naxos AudioBooks via Libby.

Frost, Robert. (1969 ed.) *The Poetry of Robert Frost: Edited by Edward Connery Lathem.* New York: Holt, Rinehart and Winston.

Goggins, David. (2018). *Can't Hurt Me: Master Your Mind and Defy the Odds.* (Sorry, APA format, but no location is printed anywhere on the book.) Lioncrest Publishing.

Hanh, Thich Nhat . (2015 ed.) *Peace is Every Step: The Path of Mindfulness in Everyday Life. Foreword by H. H. the Dalai Lama. Read by Edoardo Ballerini. Edited by Arnold Kotler.* Audiobook. Blackstone Audio, Inc. and Buck 50 Productions, LLC via Libby.

Hanson, Rick and Mendius, Richard. (2011). *Meditations to Change Your Brain.* Audiobook. Sounds True via Libby.

Hardy, Benjamin P. (2016). *How to Consciously Design Your Ideal Future.* Brooklyn, NY: Thought Catalog Books.

Hardy, Benjamin. (2020). *Personality Isn't Permanent: Break Free from Self-Limiting Beliefs and Rewrite Your Story.* New York, NY: Portfolio / Penguin (Penguin Random House LLC).

Harper, Faith G. (2018 ed.) *Unf*ck Your Brain: Using Science to Get Over Anxiety, Depression, Anger, Freak-Outs, and Triggers.* Read by the author. Audiobook. Blackstone Publishing via Libby.

Harris, Dan and Warren, Jeffrey with Adler, Carlye. (2017 ed.) *Meditation for Fidgety Skeptics. Read by Dan Harris and Jeff Warren. Unabridged.* Audiobook. Random House Audio via Libby.

Heath, Chip and Heath, Dan. (2010 ed.) *Switch: How to Change Things When Change Is Hard.* Narrated by Charles Kahlenberg. Audiobook. Random House Audio via Libby.

Irving, Washington. (ed & intro Austin McC. Fox). (1962 ed). *The Legend of Sleepy Hollow and other selections from Washington Irving: Edited and with an Introduction by Austin McC. Fox.* New York, NY: Washington Square Press (Pocket Books New York, a division of Simon & Schuster, Inc.)

Keats, John. (2007 ed.). *John Keats: Poems.* Read by Douglas Hodge. Audiobook. HighBridge Audio via Libby.

Keats, John. (2005 ed.) *Realms of Gold.* Narrated by Matthew Marsh and Samuel West. Audiobook. Naxos Audiobooks via Libby.

Kirton, Sarah. (2002) *Primstav – an ancient calendar form – The Fall Months.* Retrieved from https://norcalspelmanslag.org/ncsnlf2002/ncsnlf2002b.html

Kross, Ethan. (2021). *Chatter: The Voice in Our Head, Why It Matters, and How to Harness It.* New York, NY: Crown (Penguin Random House LLC).

Lucretius. (Ronald Melville, trans.). (2008 ed.). *On the Nature of the Universe: A verse translation by Ronald Melville, with an Introduction and Notes by Don and Peta Fowler.* Oxford, UK: Oxford University Press (Oxford World's Classics).

Macphail, Cameron. (December 21, 2020). "Winter Solstice 2020: Why do Pagans celebrate the shortest day of the year?" *The Telegraph.* Retrieved from https://www.telegraph.co.uk/christmas/2020/12/21/winter-solstice-2020-december-shortest-day-year-what-means/

Maudslay, Francesca (director). (2010). *When Rome Ruled: War Machine.* National Geographic Television, DVD. Universal City, CA: Vivendi Entertainment (Distributor).

Milton, John. (John Leonard, ed. & introd.). (2003 ed.) *Paradise Lost.* New York, NY: Penguin Books.

Ovid. (Anne & Peter Wiseman, trans, ed, & notes). (2013 ed.). *Fasti.* Oxford, UK: Oxford University Press (Oxford World's Classics).

Ovid. (trans. A.D. Melville, intro & notes E.J. Kenney; translation of "The Art of Love" by B. P. Moore with revisions by A.D. Melville). (2008 ed.) *The Love Poems.* Oxford, UK: Oxford University Press (Oxford World's Classics). [This rhyming verse translation includes all of Ovid's famous transgressive works of "love" poetry, for which he was later exiled: *Amores, Cosmetics for Ladies, Ars Amatoria,* and *Remedia Amatoria.*]

Ovid. (trans, ed, intro & notes Peter Green). (2005 ed.). *The Poems of Exile: Tristia and the Black Sea Letters, With a New Foreword; Translated with an Introduction, Notes, and Glossary by Peter Green.* Berkeley, CA: University of California Press.

Pariser, Michael. (Foreword by Robert Glover). (2020). *No More Mr. Nice Guy: The Hero's Journey: A Step-by-Step Guide to Becoming an Integrated Male.* Published by Michael Pariser, Psy.D / Michael Pariser Psychotherapy, PC via Amazon & printed in Middletown, DE.

(Various / unknown). Roebuck, Valerie J., trans. & ed.. (2010 ed.) *The Dhammapada.* New York, NY: Penguin Books (Penguin Classics & a variety of related business names).

Shakespeare, William. (2005 ed.) *The Sonnets: Read by Alex Jennings.* Audiobook. Naxos AudioBooks via Libby.

Sincero, Jen. (2017 ed.) *You Are a Badass at Making Money*. Read by Jen Sincero. Penguin Random House Audio Publishing Group: Penguin Audio via Libby.

Smith, Jesse S.. (2008). *Principles for a Self-Directed Society*. Portland, OR: Basementia Publications.

Smith, Jesse S.. (2016 ed.). *Rise of the Pagans*. Silverton, Oregon: Basementia Publications.

Stillman, Janice (editor). (2020). *The Old Farmer's Almanac: 2021*. The Old Farmer's Almanac, No. 229. Dublin, OH: Yankee Publishing, Inc. [Used to identify event dates which will become the topics of poems in early 2021.]

Sturluson, Snorri (author); Byock, Jesse L. (translation & introduction). (2005 ed.) *The Prose Edda*. New York, NY: Penguin Classics (Penguin Group (USA) Inc.).

Tennyson, Alfred. (Karen Hodder, introd. & notes). (2008 ed.) *The Works of Alfred Lord Tennyson*. Ware, Hertforshire, UK: Wordsworth Poetry Library (Wordsworth Editions Ltd.)

Thomas, Dylan. (2006 ed.). *The Essential Dylan Thomas*. Performed by Richard Burton et al. Audiobook. Naxos Audiobooks via Libby.

Tolle, Eckhart. (2005 ed.). *Practicing the Power of Now: Essential Teachings, Meditations, and Exercises from The Power of Now*. Audiobook. New World Library via Libby.

Various. (2005 ed.). *Great Narrative Poems of the Romantic Age. (John Keats, Alfred Tennyson, William Wordsworth, Samuel Taylor Coleridge, William Morris, George Crabbe)*. Narrated by John Moffatt, Samuel West, and Sarah Woodward. Audiobook. Naxos Audiobooks via Libby.

Zoll, Kenneth J. (2008). *Sinagua Sunwatchers: An Archaeoastronomy Survey of the Sacred Mountain Basin*. Sedona, AZ: Sunwatcher Publishing.

www.ingramcontent.com/pod-product-compliance
Lightning Source LLC
Chambersburg PA
CBHW021635120626
46545CB00002B/560